5 BASIC PRAYER PRINCIPLES

P. Douglas Small

Alive Publications

Except for brief quotations, no part of this publication may be reproduced, stored in a retrieval system, or transmitted in any form by any means (printed, written, photocopied, visual electronic, audio, or otherwise) without the prior permission from the publisher.

Scripture quotations, unless otherwise indicated are taken from the Holy Bible, New King James Version, Copyright – 1979, 1980, 1982, 1990, 1995, Thomas Nelson, Inc., Publishers.

ISBN: 978-0-9820115-6-0

Copyright © 2012 by Alive Publications
Kannapolis, NC 28082
All Rights Reserved
Printed in the USA

Dedication

To Bennie Triplett

My first Overseer, who believed in Barbara and I and gave us our first opportunity in full-time ministry.

And to the wonderful folks of the Dakota's

– so kind and patient in our formative learning years, some of which have remained friends for decades.

*Listen, my friend!
Your helplessness
is your best prayer.
It calls from your heart
to the heart of God with greater effect
than all your uttered pleas.
He hears it from the very moment that
you are seized with helplessness, and
He becomes actively engaged at once
in hearing and answering the prayer
of your helplessness.
Ole Kristian O. Hallesby*

Introduction

Bennie Triplett appointed me to my first church – and my second. I am sure that he may have later regretted it. I was not only green with so much to learn, but I was also a slow learner. Over the years, despite my early faltering, he has always remained gracious. He is one of the most beloved preachers in the history of the Church of God and a prolific song writer with a rich baritone voice! What a gift. He was reared at the Church of God Home for Children in Sevierville, Tennessee, now known as Smokey Mountain Children's Home.

The day the first John Deere tractor was acquired by the home, he recalls they were all so proud of it and eager to protect it. Some of the boys had never seen a tractor before, at least, one up close. Until that time, the fields of crops and vegetables used to feed the children at the home had been plowed by two teams of fine mules – Pet and Lou, and Sam and Mike. Now, with the new tractor, things would be done more effectively and efficiently. The mules could rest and so could the boys. There was new machinery. New modern

Five Basic Prayer Principles

techniques had come to the Home! Not so quick, they would soon learn.

On the first outing, the new John Deere tractor became mired axle deep in mud. Triplett recalled how enormous and powerful the tractor seemed. The two wheels were as tall as he was at the time, being some 10-11 years of age. Now those powerful wheels were halfway buried in mud. So much for new technology. There was nothing else to do, but to haul out the mules. They did.

The mules were hooked to the tractor, but they tugged and strained in vain. The tractor would not budge. Brother Eller, the Superintendent of the home, called for Tommy Pitman, one of more senior boys. He provided regular care for the mules, fed and groomed them. It was Tommy who typically put the harnesses on them, and then after a vigorous workout, he freed them to roam in the big pasture. Tommy knew those mules - better than anyone. He had a special relationship with them.

There is nothing wrong with new methods. Sometimes, when our new approaches fail, we readily fall back on old techniques. In the work of the Lord, techniques alone are never our answer. Today, there is a renewed interest in prayer – but the interest in prayer is too often as a technique, a means of church-growth, a tool for more effective evangelism, a component in some strategic process. The solution is rarely found in method

> *Our faith may be resting on a wrong basis: faith in faith or faith in prayer rather than faith in God.*
> — Ivan French

alone, it is usually in the relational. Someone has to know God, in order to know *the ways* of God.

Tommy arrived at the scene and sized up the situation. He checked the harness and tightened the trace chains. He realigned the team of mules and stroked them. And then he confidently talked them into pulling the tractor out of the axle deep mud. Triplett remembers how the situation changed when Tommy gave the command, "Pet and Lou hit the traces, the doubletree buckled, 'John Deere' and the mud gave forth a moan, and that new tractor popped up out of the muck and mire like a plastic toy."[1]

Prayer is no 'old technique' to solve some modern problem. It is not a power-tool to be used to augment a new program. It is relational, at its heart (knowing the love of God and loving Him) and at its edge (loving others into His Kingdom, into a relationship with Him). Somebody has to know God, and have a love-empowered, worshipful bond with Him. Prayer calls up power, not because prayer is powerful, but because God is powerful, and a relationship exists that engages him. Without that relationship, there is no release of power. In truth, it is not prayer that has power – none at all. It is God that has power.

A Covenant Relationship

Christian prayer is an exceptional privilege and its nature is extremely unique among religions. Muslim prayer is distinctly different than Christian prayer, as is Hindu and Buddhist prayer, not to mention pagan prayer models. God has designed prayer as the communication system specifically for those *in a covenant relationship* with Him.[2] Both testaments, old and new, are records of God's revelation, his revealing Himself to man. A testament is a covenant. So the Bible is a record of the covenant God offers man. God has a will – a plan for man. A 'will' is empowered only after the death of its maker, the Testator! We have an older will, called the Old Testament, based on the blood of bulls and goats. And we have a new will, called the New Testament. That last will and testament, offered to us by Jesus Christ, was placed into force when he died (Heb. 9:16-17). His shed blood made our relationship with the Father possible (Eph. 2:13). The New Testament, God's last will, the latest and clearest declaration of Christ's desires for us, details promises to us and the ethical principles incumbent on us, his bride, as his representative people (Mt. 5).

The environment in which God distributes gifts, things from his covenant store to us, revelation and insight, practical and material benefits, is prayer – God speaking to man and man speaking to God. God wants us to know him and to converse with him (James 4:2; John 16:24). He isn't hiding. The interactions of God with man throughout history are found in Scripture. The Bible is essentially a record of these covenants of God with mankind, through Adam and subsequently Noah. And then we have the covenant with Israel through Abraham, Moses and then David. All those have mankind in view and look to the new covenant through Jesus Christ. With each disclosure, the relationship grows. Each covenant is built on the other – the covenant with Adam, with Noah, with Abraham, that given through Moses, with David and then the new covenant

> *Effective prayer is the fruit of a relationship with God, not a technique for acquiring blessings.*
> D.A. Carson

through the blood of Jesus Christ. Each expands on the other.

We have seen prayer primarily as "asking" things of God. And certainly, making requests of God is an extraordinary privilege. But it is possible only because of our relationship with Him, through Christ (John 10:7; Mt. 11:2:3). The terms of our relationship are defined in the Bible – the Old and New Testaments. A covenant and a contract, at least from a Biblical perspective, are slightly different. A contract is largely consumed with the exchange of goods and services. If one party fails in the exchange of a payment or promises, the contract has been violated and may be broken. In a contract, cost containment and expeditious delivery of goods and services are the great concern.

A covenant, on the other hand, is not primarily about the exchange of goods and services. Rather, it is about the exchange of persons. The manager of a contract relationship may ask, "How can I get XYZ Company to do what I want them to do, what is best for me and my company, for less money and less bother?" That is the nature of a contract – it is business. And if another company can perform the services better, more efficiently, and with a cost savings, the contract is awarded to that company. That cannot describe our relationship with God. Do we switch gods when we find one who 'performs' for us more effectively or efficiently?

It should be clear that a man asking essentially the same thing about his wife would be utterly inappropriate. It would be a sign that the marriage was not healthy. The nature of the love bond in such a marriage is conditional, utilitarian. A marriage may have contractual implications, but the essence of the marriage is more covenant than contract.

Any exchange of goods and services are secondary to the relationship itself. Not so with a contract. If a man has a company and supplier who can't deliver, he finds a vendor who can provide the supplies, no matter how much he likes the previous contractor. But, we don't switch marital partners, and we don't switch gods. Those relationships are not merely contractual in nature. They are covenants – "for better or worse, richer or poorer."

> *I used to ask God to help me. Then I asked if I might help Him. I ended up by asking Him to do His work through me.*
> — Hudson Taylor

Right Promises and Right Hearts

In one of the more stunning moments in the life of Jesus, he is approached a Gentile woman who cried out first after Jesus, then after his disciples. She was desperate. But Jesus was unmoved. He displayed no typical compassion. In fact, he seemed uncharacteristically harsh. *"I was not sent except to the lost sheep of the house of Israel"* (Mt. 15:24). Bluntly, she was outside the perimeters of the covenant provisions, and he would not hear her prayer. He did eventually minister to her, but only when she acknowledged that she did not possess the rights she had implied. She had falsely represented herself as being entitled to by the use of coded language, "Son of David" (Mt. 15:22). Only with pure sincerity and honesty did Jesus respond to her. And only when she acknowledged that she was a Gentile, outside the covenant. And then, it was her pressing claim, that even Gentiles, should receive some benefit from the covenant table, that Jesus responded positively (Mt. 15:25-28).

The difference between praying and wishing is simple. Praying involves the covenant promises of God and submits to the purposes of that covenant – that all things reveal and glorify God, furthering his kingdom purposes. People who pray over an open Bible give evidence of their faith in the Covenant. They pray 'right' promises. The people whose prayers are wishful personal fancies, pray differently than those who wrestle in prayer for God's Kingdom to break into the earth, for his will to be enforced, for his heart's desire to become our heart's desire. The latter group prays out of the long covenant history of men and women who sought God's heart for their generation.

The Bible, and our covenant with God, is both the catalyst and the context for personal transformation. Prayer is the primary evidence of how vitally alive personal and corporate faith really are. People who keep talking to God over an open Bible give evidence of their faith in the covenant. Those whose prayers are wishful, personal and fanciful pray differently than those who wrestle in prayer for God's kingdom to break into the earth, for his will to be enforced, for his heart's desire to become our heart's desire. They pray out of the long covenant history of men and women who sought God's heart for their generation.

Right Faith in an Unfailing God
In Luke 18 Jesus spoke a parable about praying saying "that men always ought to pray and not lose heart" or not faint. We are not – "to not give up" on prayer. The first thing we seem to give up on is prayer! Before we stop attending worship gatherings or church activities, before we cease to listen to gospel singing or preaching, before we end evangelism

efforts and Christian education – we give up on prayer. It is always the first step to apostasy.

It is clear, the message that Jesus wants us to take away from this parable is – don't give up on prayer! Paul exhorted the Colossians in the same manner, "Continue in prayer!" (Col. 4:2)

The parable in Luke 18 involves a judge. He was not a religious man nor was he a sensitive man. He "did not fear God nor regard man" (Luke 18:2). He should not have been a judge. But he was. Before him came a woman. She was twice disadvantaged - she was a female in a man's world and she was a widow. Both were culturally and legally powerless. If she had chosen to remarry, she would have gained the protection of a new husband. But she sought a standing on her own. The idea itself was staggering. A woman passed from the control of her father to her husband, usually while still in her teens. She was, apart from father or husband, virtually without property or rights. All assets or rights were usually through a husband. The sons inherited the father's wealth. A woman shared the wealth of a husband while he was alive. When that husband died, a widow was at the mercy of her sons or her husband's brothers. Her independent rights were virtually non-existent. Her husband's land rights stayed with his family or passed to his sons while his widow might continue to be responsible for any of his debts. A widow was classed as a landless stranger – essentially the status of an immigrant.[3] This bold widow dared to appear before the Judge. She had an adversary that was creating havoc in her life, just as we do in our nemesis, Satan. She pleaded for "justice" from her adversary. It wasn't grace for which she pleaded, or even mercy. She only wanted what was due and fair to any human, justice.

Introduction

Despite the obvious oppression and the bitter state of her life, the hard-hearted insensitive judge would not intervene, at least for a while. But she was not easily dissuaded. She was persistent. She was relentless. She would not be intimidated by the resistance of the court. In every way and on a repeated basis, she brought her matter before the judge. Finally, overwhelmed by her resolve, he said within himself, "Though I do not fear God nor regard man, yet because this widow troubles me I will avenge her, lest by her continual coming she weary me." By her sheer persistence, she moves this recalcitrant, hard-hearted judge to declare relief for her. Persistence has won and she has prevailed. This is both a parable of comparison and contrast.

Jesus notes, "Hear what the unjust judge said. Shall God not avenge His own elect who cry out day and night to Him? ... He will avenge them speedily." Our God is not unjust, and on this point, is the great contrast. There is difference between our gracious God, and this hard-hearted judge. And there is a second contrast. We, the church, the corporate body of believers, are not widows. We are "the bride," the elect, the chosen of God. And our bridegroom, though presumed dead by the world, is very much alive. He is enthroned on David's throne, not in Jerusalem, but in heaven. He is King!

> *Asking with shameless persistence, the importunity that will not be denied, returns with the answer in hand.*

The text instructs – When heaven does not respond, don't draw harsh conclusions about God. Persist in prayer.

Five Basic Prayer Principles

Don't give up. And second, remember your standing as the 'bride-partner' of the living Christ, raised from the dead. What could be impossible for him? What prayer could he not answer? Refuse, as did this widow, to see yourself as powerless.

"Nevertheless, when the Son of Man comes, will He really find faith on the earth?" In the middle of the verse 8, there is a dramatic turn. The question posed by Jesus seems utterly out of place. What possible connection could this eschatological question have to do with this parable? It may be the most profound insight of all. Very simply, the survival of faith on the earth is rooted in persistent prayer. Not in open churches or an underground movement due to persecution. Not in the operation of our Christian Colleges, our Seminaries or other Christian enterprise operations – but simply in a praying people.

Principle One
Prayer is Perplexing

Our ordinary views of prayer are not found in the New Testament.

We look upon prayer as a means for getting something for ourselves; the Bible idea of prayer is that we may get to know God Himself.

Oswald Chambers

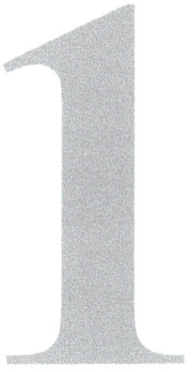

A God Who is Not Pragmatic

In a "science-soaked" culture, prayer is something we struggle to comprehend. We want to see it as pragmatic, to understand its "workings" rather than rest in the relationship itself. Einstein is said to have been asked near the end of his life if there were other arenas that he would have liked to have pursued, other mysteries that he would like to have unraveled. Einstein's response was simply that someone needed to "check out prayer!" There is a power attached to prayer. And yet it cannot be understood in a mere cause-effect manner. Prayer is mystery, because God is mysterious. So, prayer doesn't collaborate well with science. It is essentially relational. It is an interaction between unpredictable people and an utterly reliable, but mystifying God. Depend on Him, but don't dictate His course of action. Bank on His provision, but don't calculate His ways and means so as to reduce Him to a puppet. Count on an answer, but be prepared for one different than you might have anticipated. He demands His role as God. He is not interested in switching positions with us as the Lords, and him as servant. Prayer is not a bell that he answers.

Five Basic Prayer Principles

Richard Foster believes,

> Our problem is that we assume prayer is something to master the way we master algebra or auto mechanics. That puts us in the "on top" position, where we are competent and in control. But when praying, we come "underneath" where we calmly and deliberately surrender the control and become incompetent ... the truth of the matter is, we all come to prayer with a tangled mass of motives altruistic and selfish, merciful and hateful, loving and bitter. Frankly, this side of eternity we will never unravel the good from the bad, the pure from the impure. God is big enough to receive us with all our mixture. That is what grace means, and not only are we saved by it we live by it as well. And we pray by it.[4]

Prayer is perplexing, because it is tied to the heart of a God whose ways are past finding out, whose foolishness is beyond our collective human wisdom. Grace, not technique, makes our prayer life successful. God's goodness, not our good praying, is the driving force behind prayer's answers (Mt. 7:11; James 1:17). And yet, prayer is the very process by which he changes and alters us.

A Culture that is Not a Praying Culture

Perhaps, in part, because of our cultural baptism in pragmatism and predictable outcomes, we have drifted from prayer. Whatever the reason, it is clear now that we are not a praying culture. The Hindu culture is a praying culture. The Buddhist culture is a praying culture. If you travel to the Middle East and are in any Muslim area when the call to prayer is given, you will watch grown, strong men, fall to their knees, bow their faces to the ground and pray to Allah.

The same is true of Jews. On any El AL flight to Jerusalem, Orthodox Jews will crowd to the eastern end of the jet come sunrise for a time of prayer. With a prayer book in hand and a talit over their head, they will pray openly in the aisle of the plane. No shame. No dishonor. No reticence. They will stand openly at the Wailing Wall in Jerusalem and wail! Majority World Christian cultures are full of praying people. America is not a praying culture. It has increasingly become an anti-prayer culture. We have allowed a legal war on public prayer to prevail in our nation. We continue to systematically remove all public liberty in the area of prayer, particularly Christian prayer, specifically prayer in the name of Jesus. Samuel Chadwick believed prayer should be pervasive, "There is nothing about which I do not pray. I go over all my life in the presence of God. All my problems are solved there."[5]

Churches that Do Not Pray
Not only is America not a praying culture, but America's church is not a praying church. The average American church member prays four minutes a day. And most of that, I jokingly add, is for a parking place near the door at the neighborhood Wal-Mart. A survey taken in a church in Alberta, Canada asked this question: What kind of prayer life do you have? Are you a crisis pray-er? A casual pray-er? Or a committed pray-er? Of 300 responses, 276 classified themselves as crisis or casual pray-ers. Only 24 or 8 percent met the criteria of being a committed person of prayer.

The theology books of the 1970's and 1980's almost never mention prayer, at least in a direct way. Prayer has been ignored by our culture and ignored by the North American Church. Until a few years ago, only one American seminary taught a class on prayer. Most Bible Colleges and Seminaries do not even classify prayer as a theological item. It is seen, if at all, as a mere component of discipleship or Christian Ministries.

A survey of 572 United States pastors demonstrated that 57 percent prayed less than 20 minutes a day. That means that the total time spent in prayer, in communion and consultation with God by American pastors is just over two hours per week. Another 34 percent of American pastors pray for 20 minutes or more per day, but less than an hour per day. The average time spent in prayer by American pastors is 22 minutes per day – 2.5 hours per week. An average of twenty-two minutes a day for those who are the spiritual guides of the faithful and the leaders of moral renewal for the nation. In Australia the average is 23 minutes. In New Zealand, it is 30 minutes. In Japan, hardly a Christian nation, it is a surprising 44 minutes and in Korea, it is 90 minutes a day. [6]

> *It is a tremendously hard thing to pray aright, yea, it is verily the science of all sciences.*
> Martin Luther

A Practice So Little Understood

Why do we ignore prayer? It seems that prayer is so contrary to our utilitarian, pragmatic way of approaching life in America. We are an action-oriented culture. Our sports and entertainment options demand excitement. Television turns a scene every few seconds. Lifetimes are collapsed into short reviews. Complex mysteries are solved in an hour with time for dramatic commercials. In comparison, we may see no immediate and measurable results from private and quiet seasons of prayer. So we conclude that it is a nice thing, a noble thing, a sweet thing – but not a fundamentally essential thing. That is not what Scripture indicates. It is not what we know deep in our hearts. But it is the net result of our practice.

Prayer, it turns out, is the consistently untested and untried element in our American ministries. We bake our spiritual cakes without it and the taste seems the same. It isn't the same! The problem is our almost complete loss of discernment. We think of prayer like we think about the human appendix or the tonsils, you can live with them or without them. And life seems to go on just the same – maybe better. At any rate, we treat prayer like an option. A pastor told me recently, "I had never considered prayer that important until I heard you passionately talk about it." This Pentecostal pastor admitted that he needed to go home and reconsider the importance of prayer. The Scripture considers prayer as indispensable. If spirit is breath to us, then prayer is breathing. There is no life in the body of Christ without it. No true life!

It is true that prayer is somewhat of a mystery. We pray, and nothing seems to happen. Then things happen that cannot be traced to any specific prayer. That mystifies us. We make a particular request of God in prayer, and instead of getting what we had asked for, we get something completely different. At times, it is something wonderful, something that we would have ever dared to ask of God. We get the unstated desire of our hearts. At other times, the answer seems to disappoint us – at least for a season. Then one day, we have an *"aha!"* moment. Looking back, we realize that if we had gotten what we had requested, it would not have been in our best interest. Instead, our path took a different turn. It was a confusing season at first, disappointing us in an acute way, but in time we see the truth of Romans 8:28.

God was working in our lives in ways that we could not have understood then, even if an angel had been sent to have coffee with us and explain God's plan.

Prayer is not about directing God. It is not about moving his hand. Requests and petitions are legitimate components of prayer. Desire for counsel and wisdom, for direction and clarity are what sometimes drive us into encounters with God in prayer. But prayer is not exchanging information with God. Or printing out the directions for our lives for the next day or week. It is not a Christian's substitute for a horoscope.

A Relational Perspective Ignored
Like the covenant, prayer is relational. It is not a conversation over a contract. Not a dispute over mere stuff. It is the affirmation of our trust in God and his word. It is a celebration of our faith, an action that says daily, by the investment our time, that He is involved in our lives even if in sometimes invisible and undetectable ways. It is the tender evidence that we believe in His love and grace. The power of prayer is not in our words, it is when something deep inside of us touches something deep inside of God – and we know that we know that He is there. Trust, in such moments, is complete. And in such moments, we are certain everything will be all right. Such occasions defy words. They cannot always be translated conceptually or expressed verbally.

However, this is not a mere "feeling" that we are describing. It is more than emotion. It is spirit. It has a texture beyond emotion. It has life about it. Life that is bigger than we can produce in and of ourselves. We have entered in such moments into the arena of God's presence by the mystery of prayer and we are sensing His power and presence.

A Transformational Dynamic that is Resisted

So prayer is the context in which we honor and sustain our covenantal relationship with God. E. Stanley Jones said:

> In prayer you align yourself to the purpose and power of God and His is able to do things through you that you could not otherwise do ... for this is an open universe, where some things are left open, contingent upon our doing them ... and they will never be done except as we pray.

That is a fascinating quote. Jones argues that prayer is an "aligning" experience. Something imperceptible happens to us as we prayer. It is not so much God that is changed by our prayer or moved by it. We are moved. And we are strangely moved in a way that reorders us, bringing us under His sovereign custody. Without this alignment, this change in us and our relationship with God by the process of prayer, there are things that God could not and would not do through us. Of course, it is not God that is limited by our lack of prayer. We are limited in terms of participation in His work by our lack of prayer.

Jones goes so far as to argue that "some things will never be done except as we pray." He offers us the idea of an "open" universe, a concept that suggest that the sovereign God has left some ends to our discretion and yet simultaneously subordinate to participation with Him in prayer. He could but He will not. Mysteriously, He has yielded some things to the persistence of man in the discipline of prayer. It turns out, "God governs the world by prayer!"

Prayer – The Essential for Appropriations from God

Andrew Murray says,

> God's intense longing to bless seems to be graciously limited by His dependence upon intercession ... God regards intercession as the highest expression of His people's readiness to receive and yield themselves wholly to the working of His almighty power.[7]

In a similar vein, Andrew Murray notes that the blessings of God themselves are accessed only through prayer. James agrees,

> *"You have not, because ye ask not!" (James 4:2)*

But again, prayer is not a mere means of "withdrawing grace" from the believer's heavenly account. James warns that prayer stubbornly yields blessings if we utilize it to "consume" it upon our lusts. And Murray notes that the response of God in blessing is not merely to prayer itself, but to what is happening to us and in us by the experience of prayer. Intercession is an "expression of readiness" to receive and yield. Here is the idea of alignment again, expressed in a different way. Murray observes that all of this is happening in order that we might be available to be used of God, to participate "wholly" in the "working of God's almighty power."

Prayer is the context in which God changes us in order that He might work in us and through us to accomplish His purposes and fulfill our destiny. The power of prayer is found in the way that prayer transforms us and makes us available to be used of God. Its efficacy is not in well-formed phrases. It is not our impressive grasp of theology expressed heavenward. It is not inspiring liturgy. The power and effectiveness of our prayer is in something deeper. It is not our strength in prayer but our weakness openly declared before our Father, God. It is the place when we at the end our self, our own resources and solutions wrap up in faith, and cry out to God. That is when prayer is most effective.

Principle Two
Prayer Should be Purifying

*What is the reason that some believers
are so much brighter
and holier than others?
I believe the difference in nineteen
cases out of twenty, arises from
different habits about private prayer.
I believe that those who are not
eminently holy pray little and those
who are eminently holy pray much.*

James Charles – J. C. Ryle

On the bumper of the car was a fish – a Christian symbol. And in the symbol, was the word "Jesus." Here was a born-again, "Jesus" loving kind of Christian. On the other side of the car's bumper was another sticker, a dove. Ah, a Spirit-filled Christian. On the back window was the decal of a Christian college. So, my friend reasoned, here was a born-again, Spirit-filled believer, who had attended a Christian college. He could be a preacher! Getting even closer, there was an air-freshener hanging from the rear-view mirror. Unbelievable. Unreal. Puzzling. It was the silhouette of a playboy-bunny.

Winston Churchill once declared that England needed "... a supreme recovery of moral health and martial vigor." America now seems to be in the same place, lacking in both moral clarity of values and force of character. Dr. Erwin W. Lutzer, Senior Pastor of Chicago's Moody Church observed that the evangelical ship is taking on water. He cautions, "The church cannot be inundated by worldly values and yet meet its responsibility of keeping society from decay. If our assignment is to reclaim the moral ground of this nation for righteousness, how can we do it if we ourselves are guilty of the same sins?" Only if we are "brought to our knees,

God may begin to give us spiritual victories that could stem abortion, infanticide and drug abuse ... The greatest need for the church today is believing prayer."

Over 90 percent of American's say that they pray, at least on some occasions. But less than 50 percent in any region of the United States, including the deeply religious south and the conservative mid-west, pray about the moral choices they make in life. We have developed a kind of wall of separation between the help we ask of God, and the foul lines of morality. Prayer should be a purifying experience. Talking to and fellowshipping with a Holy God should change us. Charles Spurgeon declared, "God visits every house where night and morning prayers are made, but where these are neglected, sin is incurred."[8]

Re-Creating God and Faith

We have developed for ourselves a "nurturing faith" that is too often detached from the concept of God's holiness and our sinful condition. We have recreated God. We have fixed in our minds the limiting image and perception of Him as helper. He is a "very present" help in trouble (Psalm 46:10). Indeed, we are told, *"Call upon the Lord in the time of trouble"* and he would deliver (Psalm 50:15; 86:7).

But we are also reminded that the deliverance provides the opportunity for us to glorify Him (Psa. 50:15). And that requires a qualified and credible witness. In the day of Jeremiah, the Lord instructed him to inform the people that God would not hear (Jeremiah 11:14), and that his refusal was traceable to their moral and spiritual rebellion. They had disqualified themselves as witnesses in God's behalf. Such a message was no more popular then, than it is now. Jeremiah was censored and placed in prison for his blunt and politically incorrect speech.

Our culture wants love, but without truth. We are open to his affirmation, but resistant to conviction, to moral transformation. This notion of a "nurturing faith" which does not demand lifestyle change or moral-purity with personal discipline is immensely popular, if not pervasive in the church today. But it is not a Biblical notion at all. Biblical prayer is transformational. Love constrains. It does not offer a lower standard than the law, but one that is higher (Mt. 5:17-20). Our righteousness must exceed that of the Scribes and Pharisees. We are called to adopt the model of the Father – to be perfect, whole, growing toward maturity (Mt. 5:48).

The nature of our covenant with God is not merely to allow us to access grace, as if it were a free divine ATM card to be used recklessly. And here is the mystery – grace is free. And it is unlimited. And it is be lavishly applied to sinful hearts. And yet, grace is not cheap. Nor is it the ultimate gift God wants to give us. Grace is a means to the end. It is both space and energy. First, it is the relational space in which a holy God works with and in sinners. It is the arena in which he transforms sinners into saints. Second, grace is also the energy that drives that transforming process by which he changes us to sons and daughters, and then uses us in mission.

Prayer as Transformation – Not Merely a Transaction
Prayer cannot be perceived as merely "doing business" with God. It is not primarily transactional. Again, it is transformation. *We* seek the *hand* of God. We want that Divine hand to perform in our behalf. God seeks to place us in His hand. He longs for us to seek "his face." For in

seeing His face, we are moved at the very core of our being. An encounter with the sovereign God of Scripture will not and cannot leave you and me the same.

Here is the idea of *incarnation*. God seeks to change us in order that he might be revealed in us and *through* us. A part of that transformation is the impartation of his holiness and our resultant sensitivity to purity. Prayer should be a purifying experience.

> *Prayer will promote our personal holiness as nothing else, except the study of the Word of God.*

A Humbling Encounter
The scripture says:

> *Submit yourselves therefore to God. Resist the devil, and he will flee from you (James 4:6).*

There is no place where we more clearly submit to God following the master's example than in prayer – "Not my will, but your will be done!" Notice that "resistance" to the devil and "submission" to God are parallel processes. Our capacity to resist in an overcoming way is connected to our submission. Satan flees not due to the personal force of our resistance, but due to the level of our submission! It is not us that he fears. It is the One to whom we are submitted. He would devour us, but we are under the shadow of the One whose mere breath will destroy him (II Thess. 2:8). Lone rangers who pretend to be spiritual Rambo's may go about the country wielding their personal spiritual power, screaming at the darkness, but it is the quiet and humble servant that is the most effective slayer of the dragon. The Devil runs from such saints – behind them is God, terrible and awesome.

Imagine an enemy, spotting a victim, his prey, and closing in for the kill. Suddenly the victim bends downward and bows toward the ground. To the predator, it is unclear what his actions mean or what his intent might be. Momentarily, there is a pause in the action. And then, behind the supposed victim is the predator's own nemesis, his most deadly enemy. Suddenly, the battle shifts. The hunter is now threatened. He has pursued his victim only to run blindly into a trap, face to face, with his own worst enemy. His only option is retreat. He must flee. We "submit to God" and "resist the Devil" and he flees. Not by our power, but because of the One who is 'always with us.'

> *Humble yourselves in the sight of the Lord, and he shall lift you up. (James 4:10)*

Exaltation comes from God. And humility is the condition that allows God to raise us up. Pride brings the resistance of God. But humility is the requisite for being given a trust by God. No clearer role is there for prayer than that of humbling us!

A Purifying Experience
Augustine prayed,

> Breath in me, O Holy Spirit, that my thoughts may all be holy. Act in me, O Holy Spirit, that my work, too, may be

> *A holy life does not live in the closet, but it cannot live without the closet.*
> *E. M. Bounds*

holy. Draw my heart, O Holy Spirit, that I love but what is holy. Strengthen me, O Holy Spirit, to defend all that is holy. Guard me, then, O Holy Spirit, that I always may be holy.

Augustine believed prayer challenged and changed our thought-life. It impacted our actions. It sanctified our work. It redirected our affections. It infused us with Divine might. It made us vigilant defenders of the Sacred. And it invited the God, the Holy Spirit, to hedge us in, that we might fulfill God's purposes in a worthy manner.

Draw nigh to God, and he will draw nigh to you. Cleanse your hands, ye sinners; and purify your hearts, ye double minded (James 4:8).

The experience of prayer – "draw near to God" - is again referenced. We demonstrate the discipline by coming near to Him by prayer. And when we do, He comes near to us! Such a process, James declares, results in other changes. When God comes near – hands must be cleansed. If we are to touch Him, it must be with holy hands. If we are to handle holy things, our hands must be sanctified. If the people we touch are not to be contaminated, we must touch them in holy ways with pure hands. When God comes near – hands and hearts must be pure. God discerns the things that are hidden to others. An impure heart is the source of a double-mind. Indecision is rooted in a polluted heart. And an unchanged heart is one that has not been challenged by the presence of God in prayer. Transformational prayer.

An Integrity Builder

Confess your faults one to another, and pray one for another, that ye may be healed. James 5:16

Rarely do most churches experience an authentic confessional environment. We may move through a liturgy of confession and offer one another "the blessing" of peace, but we rarely experience the tear-stained, heart-felt, humbling and unifying confessional environment that is in view here. And the context is that of prayer. Here is genuine openness and transparent honesty. Here, with our flaws unhidden, yet not flaunted, we are in pursuit of God and His healing hand. The whole church wants to be healed, and it must realize that something is preventing that wholeness. It cannot be merely the physical that James has in mind here. There is more. Prayer creates an atmosphere that encourages candor with trust, vulnerability and personal growth. In prayer, I see myself as undone (Isa. 6), and I simultaneously long to be healed. It is in this prayerful environment that healing power is released. In this environment, honesty is exhibited before God and one another, and then wrapped in prayer. And the power of God comes.

Ole Hallesby believed,

> When we go to our meeting with God, we should go like a patient to his doctor, first to be thoroughly examined and afterwards to be treated for our ailment. Then something will happen when you pray.[9]

We have people today who want to be healed, but they will not allow themselves to come into a place of open and honest self-examination. It is not the typical prayer request that is being exchanged here. This is not confession of physical maladies or aches and pains. This is a confession of faults. The Greek word is *paraptoma*, (par-ap'-to-mah). It means a side-slip, a lapse or deviation whether it was unintentional error or willful transgression. It can also mean a fall – as in a moral fall, some character fault, some persistent offence, or it may mean sin or trespass. This is not what we typically confess to one another.

In fact, discretion and social training encourage us to "hide such things." Pride demands that we do so. But in prayer – in the moments when we meet Divine Holiness – we are moved into disclosure. Suddenly, the context of corporate prayer becomes confessional. In honesty before God, coupled with brokenness and prayer one for another, the power of God is released to begin to heal us.

Why are their so many sick among us? Why do we not see healing power? Is the day of miracles over? Is it a lack of faith? Perhaps it is because we want healing but we do not want the humility required to confess our faults, the shame of the public admission that we are not all we appear to be. Bound by our pride, we retain the hidden sin of our hearts. We remain tight-lipped and we consequently seal ourselves off from the healing power of God.

The Power of Righteousness

> *The effectual fervent prayer of a righteous man availeth much.*

James (5:16) says it is the energized prayer – the effectually fervent prayer – of a "righteous" man that is effective. Prayer is the environment that keeps us righteous. And it is a process that demands our sensitivity to righteousness or it will be a futile exercise.

The Psalmist declared:

If I regard iniquity in my heart, the Lord will not hear me (Psalm 66:18).

Iniquity. Here is another demand for purity and righteousness. The Hebrew word for "regarding" iniquity is *ra'ah*, (raw-aw') which means to see or to recognize. It may also mean to approve of, to behold in an admiring way. It can even mean to enjoy. God is saying,

> *Believing prayer from a wholly-cleansed heart never fails.*
> The Kneeling Christian

"If you can see iniquity inside yourself, don't expect me to hear you." Or, "If you are going to talk with me, you have to put that away. I will not allow you to simultaneously experience iniquity, or gaze at it, or enjoy it in any way, and talk with me at the same time." God insists that I must respect His holiness. There is to be a reverence for and of His purity that impacts me. Changes me.

In one of the most frequently quoted passages of the Old Testament we hear:

> *If my people, which are called by my name, shall humble themselves, and pray, and seek my face, and turn from their wicked ways; then will I hear from heaven, and will forgive their sin, and will heal their land. II Chronicles 7:14.*

J. C. Ryle asked:

> What is the reason that some believers are so much brighter and holier than others? I believe the difference in nineteen cases out of twenty, arises

from different habits about private prayer. I believe that those who are not eminently holy pray little and those who are eminently holy pray much.[10]

Jerry Bridges noted:

> Many Christians have what we might call a "cultural holiness". They adapt to the character and behavior pattern of Christians around them. As the Christian culture around them is more or less holy, so these Christians are more or less holy. But God has not called us to be like those around us. He has called us to be like himself. Holiness is nothing less than conformity to the character of God.[11]

C. S. Lewis said, "No clever arrangement of rotten eggs ever makes a good omelet." If God is going to serve us up to a watching world as a sweet-smelling savor, then we must be pure. And that means transformational time in the presence of a holy God.

Bonhoeffer lamented, "One is distressed by the failure of reasonable people to perceive either the depths of evil or the depths of the holy."[12] The result is always compromise and spiritual lethargy. Prayer, real prayer, involves personal conferences with a holy God

> *Walking with God down the avenue of prayer we acquire something of His likeness, and unconsciously we become witnesses to others of His beauty and His grace.*
> — E. M. Bounds

that produce holiness and purity of heart. Sadly, good people are kept from prayer and repentance. They come to depend on their own moral strength – but these are moralists, not Christians, even if they speak 'christianese.' Bad people, that is, people who lack moral character of the Biblical genre in their lives, and simultaneously want to avoid moral change, often resent the public admission of such values fearing their implications or imposition. They consider themselves free and intellectual – even though they are fervently and frantically falling into reactionary patterns against things they say they disbelieve. Their obsession is proof of the moral power of Biblical values themselves.

Tragically, both good and bad people avoid the very thing that makes a good Christian – dependence on God. "The essence of chastity is not the suppression of lust, but the total orientation of one's life towards a goal."[13] God is not looking for perfection! He is looking for integrity and dependence on him. Grace hems us in to true righteousness – the righteousness of Christ.

Principle Three
Prayer Alters Our Perspective

The secret of failure is that we see men rather than God. Romanism trembled when Martin Luther saw God.
The 'great awakening' sprang into being when Jonathan Edwards saw God. The world became the parish of one man when John Wesley saw God. Multitudes were saved when Whitfield saw God. Thousands of orphans were fed when George Muller saw God. And He is 'the same yesterday, today, and forever.' "

3

Catherine Marshall said, "One can believe in the divinity of Jesus Christ and feel no personal loyalty to Him at all - indeed, pay no attention whatever to His commandments and His will for one's life."[14] That, of course, is possible only in a cool, distant and intellectual sense. It is not Biblical Christianity. True discipleship calls us out of our narrow world and forces us to embrace a global challenge.

William Carey was a shoe cobbler before he was a missionary. As he labored each day, he kept beside him, on his workbench, a map of the world. He prayed and worked – and worked and prayed. As he worked, he prayed over the world. And God called him to reach that world.[15] That is missions' history! Had his prayer experience been narrow, he might have remained a shoemaker. Instead he impacted a nation, and became an icon of inspiration for a veritable army of missionaries. What destiny is the lack of prayer keeping you from?

The Disciple's Request: Lord, Teach Us To Pray
Of all the things the disciples might have asked for, what they requested was that Jesus teach them to pray. It was not for

instructions on more effective teaching or preaching, healing or doing miracles. They did not ask for "water walking" lessons. They asked for instruction on prayer. Why? It was obviously clear to them that the power in the earthly ministry of Jesus – in all he did, teaching, preaching, healing, miracles, and wisdom – was from his life of prayer. His communion with the Father, brought forth the Father's glory.

At night when they were ready to turn in, he was still out somewhere in prayer. In the morning when they arose, he had already slipped away to some quiet place for prayer (Mk. 1:35). On some occasions, he spent the entire night in prayer (Luke 6:12). Jesus did not pray to do ministry. His ministry was prayer. He moved from one place of prayer to another with the glory and power of the Father God flowing out of Him. We focus on what happened in between the prayer sessions of Jesus

> *Is the Son of God praying in me, or am I dictating to Him?... Getting things from God ... is a most initial form of prayer; prayer is getting into perfect communion with God. If the Son of God is formed in us by regeneration, He will press forward in front of our common sense and change our attitude to the things about which we pray.*
>
> Oswald Chambers

– the teaching, preaching, ministry, miracles. Things that were obvious. But all of that was possible because of the unobvious, his secret life of prayer. He came to the earth to pray. He was an intercessor. The ultimate intercessor. And he ever lives today to make intercession (Heb. 7:25).

The Lord's Response: The Model Prayer
"Teach us to pray!" the disciples asked him. His response was incredibly simple. We call the words that follow "The Lord's Prayer." His prayer is actually found in John 17. The so-called 'Lord's Prayer' might be more properly called "the disciple's prayer" for it is the model he gave us for prayer (Lk. 11:2-4; Mt. 9:9-13).

After this manner therefore pray ye:

Our Father which art in heaven, Hallowed be thy name.

Thy kingdom come. Thy will be done in earth, as it is in heaven.

Give us this day our daily bread.

And forgive us our debts, as we forgive our debtors.

And lead us not into temptation, but deliver us from evil:

For thine is the kingdom, and the power, and the glory, for ever. Amen. (Matthew 6:9-13).

Notice, this prayer begins with God. "Our Father ... your name is holy ... let your kingdom come and your will be done." This prayer ends, "For thine (Father) is the kingdom, power and glory, for ever!" So the prayer begins and ends with a focus upon God and his Kingdom. It begins with a focus upon his will and not the imposition of mine upon Him by prayer. How does your prayer begin and end?

The End Result: An Altered Perspective
Prayer is a means by which God expands and stretches my perspective. He wants me to see the world as he sees it. So in prayer, we are pulled from the dusty earth to the celestial heaven. We are graciously forced to seek His will and not our own. We catch glimpses through the telescope of time and see eternal implications in what we do, so that our decisions are not rooted in some narrow slice of time that will affect us negatively for all eternity. We are moved out of our narrow little world, and into a larger arena. We are mentored to think relationally, not selfishly and independently.

Watch the movement:

From	**To**
Cosmic orphans	Members of the Father's family
Earth	Heaven
Our frailty	His Hallowedness and Wholeness
My domain	His Kingdom
My best wisdom	His will
My directing Him	My surrender to Him
Me	We
Us	Our
Merely begin forgiven	Becoming forgiving
Avoiding temptation	Being liberated from Evil
Now	Eternity

Prayer should change our perspective. God wants to inflame our praying. Christ gave us *all authority*. Our mission involves *all nations* - the whole world. As we go we are to observe *all commands* – that means that our mission involves a well-planned strategy. The uncompleted mission given to the church by Christ is for *all time* – "Lo, I am with you always, even to the end of the age" (Mt. 28:20). God is waiting for some generation, at some point in time, to take seriously all the authority, all his commands, and in faith, to strategically fulfill the mission to reach all nations.[16]

The New Focus: Prayer Re-centers Us

So much of our prayer begins and ends with us. Ultimately, prayer is not about us. It is about God. Of course "our stuff" is included, because God cares about us. We may ask about "daily bread." We may request "forgiveness of our debts." We may even ask God to exempt us from "temptation and tests," to guard our day so that we do not encounter evil and the Evil One. And yet, we are never instructed to make even these types of requests in the singular.

Not once can we pray using this model – *"me," "my"* or *"I."* The prayer that Jesus

> *Prayer meetings are dead affairs when they are merely asking sessions; there is adventure, hope and life when they are believing sessions, and the faith is corporately, practically and deliberately affirmed.*
>
> Norman Grubb

taught us begins and ends with God. Prayer must alter our focus. It isn't the attempt to get God to focus on us, as much as it is to see Him – as Father, as King, as head of a universal and unstoppable, incomparable Kingdom, as the One who fills the heavens, the earth being too small for Him. As the One who supplies needs, because of his unlimited creative capacity, and guides because of His omniscient oversight of all, and delivers due to his omnipotent and unequaled power. Prayer must shift our focus from our narrow slice of pain, to see Him. Such a shift in focus takes the spotlight off our problems and causes us to see the solution. Only with a "God-focus" are our problems manageable.

The Enlarged Community: Relational Awareness
The prayer that we are given as a model is devoid of narrow personal language, and loaded with corporate and relational language - *"Our," "Us," and "We."* In asking for daily bread, I must request it for "us." In requesting forgiveness, I must do so with a concern for broader relationships. Only as I am willing to forgive, do I experience the full power of God's forgiveness. God will not allow a mere *transaction* with Him, He is interested in our *transformation.*

Not only has the focus shifted from us, and our pain, to God. It is also broadened to include others. Prayer can't be a constricted and limited transaction between "me and God." Prayer constantly stretches me to be as inclusive and loving as the God to whom I pray. It alters my language from me, to us. It enlarges my focus from self, to community. It reminds me that the Father has endowed me with brothers – this is a family.

Prayer is about relationships:

- The relationship with God _as Father_ – "Our Father."
- The relationship with God _as King_ of the kingdom – "for thine is the kingdom."
- The relationship with God as _the architect of divine purpose_ in our lives – "thy will be done."
- The relationship with God _as provider_ – "give us our daily bread." The phrase "our daily bread" may also be an allusion to the request for "daily provision" typical for the Roman military officer at the beginning of each day. His request and the subsequent supply obligated him to go in the strength of that bread in service to the Emperor.
- The relationship with God _as Judge_ who releases us legally from our moral debt and its consequences – "forgive us our debts."
- The relationship with God _as guide and protector_ – "lead us not into temptation!" He leads us. He is active in helping us navigate the bends and turns in the road.
- The relationship with God _as warrior_ – "deliver us!" He delivers us. His hand has gotten us liberty and victory.
- The relationship with _the God of power and glory!_

If prayer became the daily reminder of these simple relationships with God, our lives would be changed. "Most men pray for power, the strength to do things. Few people pray for love, the quality to be someone," observes Robert D. Foster.

At the heart of the prayer is the relational core –

- Care for the *physical* needs of others: bread;
- Care for the *psychological* health of one another:

- forgiveness;
- And care for the *spiritual purity and liberty* from the corrupting grip of the Tempter: the spiritual dimension.

It's all here. We are to give to others. We are to feed the hungry – and this is something that can't simply be institutionalized. Furthermore, since giving "daily bread" to others is something we are to pray about, it cannot be an act of cool detached care. The greater gift to those who are hungry is not edible manna, but spiritual bread. We must pray for them. Prayer and care are welded together here. Care is a way of acting out our prayer for another. So James would forbid us from praying and blessing the needy by saying, "Go, I wish you well; keep warm and well fed," while we do nothing about the physical need. James asked, "What good is that?" (James 2:16). Prayer moves us to act. And yet, action without prayer is simply that - human action, without spiritual conviction. This kind of prayer makes every believer a missionary.

Forgiveness is the priestly and pastoral dimension of prayer. Someone has said, "Resentment is like a glass of poison that a man drinks; then he sits down and waits for his enemy to die." Jesus said,

> "Settle matters quickly with your adversary who is taking you to court. Do it while you are still with him on the way, or he may hand you over to the judge, and the judge may hand you over to the officer, and you may be thrown into prison. I tell you the truth, you will not get out until you have paid the last penny" (Mt. 5:25).

This is a practical piece of advice, but buried here are profound spiritual truths as well. Before you leave another person, after there has been some type of rift in the relationship, create conciliatory ground. Come to agreement – *"Agree with your adversary"* in part or whole. In doing so, you neutralize the conflict, which only multiplies, sometimes both irrationally and exponentially, with the separation of the two parties. Unity pacifies. It appeases. It placates. It mollifies. It soothes. It aborts war and acrimony.

There are four phases to the crumbling relationship here –

- First, a friend has become an adversary. Something has happened to damage the relationship. The division intensifies and is considered unresolvable by the two parties alone. Their absence from one another exacerbates the issue.
- Now, to settle the conflict, a third party is needed, thus judicial action. The problem is going to be adjudicated in court.
- Third, an arrest is made. Guilt is determined.
- Fourth, one of the parties loses his freedom. Placed in prison, he is no longer at liberty. He is in lock-down.

Hidden in the text is a spiritual description of what happens to an infected relationship when there is no forgiveness. Here is the scenario.

- Two people disagree. The quarrel becomes adversarial. The distance between intensifies and they fail to come to any kind of agreement. They part company with the division firmly in place.
- The matter ends up in God's court! Heaven pays

attention to division – God hates discord. One brother may press the matter before God in prayer, eager to resolve the matter. But the failure to be open to reconciliation and forgiveness peaks God's attention.
- One party bears the greater guilt before God. The Holy Spirit pursues one, and then the other, with conviction. But there is no tender heart of repentance, no openness to change, no willingness to forgive.
- Suddenly, the relationship is in lock-down. It is no longer free, no longer full of joy. Neither party feels liberty toward or around the other. One, or perhaps both, are now in bondage. The rift may affect families, a whole church, a city or even nations.

In bondage, there is no freedom – to fellowship or to love, to forgive or receive forgiveness. Under conviction, and simultaneously resistant to it, refusing to bend or break before God or the offended brother, the heart grows hard. Rationalizations deepen. Sensitivity to the Spirit is affected. Instead of being the Comforter, the Spirit was sent to be (Phil. 2:1-4; II Cor. 7:6; Isa. 61:1), He is forced to correct a resistant saint (John 16:8). In truth, it is worse than all that.

One or both parties have placed themselves in harm's way. They have chosen to act in ways that God has chosen to judge. While he loves, he will not exempt even his children from the consequences of their actions. Grace does not suspend sin's toxic effects. I must not act in ways that God has determined to judge! Doing so, I am clearly in sin and potentially face some type of consequence from the principle of judgment built into all sin. All of this is due to my failure "agree quickly" and avert an adversarial relationship. In short, the failure to forgive. Nothing furthers psychological health more than forgiving and being forgiven.

What keeps us from pursuing peace, from bearing the olive branch, from first asking for forgiveness? It is usually pride! "Excessive pride, the seat of so much misery and unhappiness, like resentment, results from an inflated ego crying for recognition. Criticism hurts us because we allow too much self to come to the fore."[17] And that causes us to become stiff and unbending, unforgiving and revenge seeking. "Prayer," on the other hand, "helps us step outside ourselves. It is not the "precious self" that needs to be eradicated, but the "egotistical self". After all, "a person wrapped up in himself is a pretty small package."[18]

> *The one thing above all others that bolts and bars the way into the "presence chamber's of prayer is unwillingness to forgive from the heart.*
> Samuel Chadwick

> "A Christian will find it cheaper to pardon than to resent. Forgiveness saves the expense of anger, the cost of hatred, and the waste of spirit." Hannah More

Forgiveness is not the dismissal of the wrong. It is the sanity that says the past, no matter how hurtful and disillusioning, can't be changed. And it is giving up my right to hurt another for hurting me. It is refusing to be a part of continuing the war. It is the call for a truce, on the spot, then and there.

"Not to forgive is to be imprisoned by the past, by

old grievances that do not permit life to proceed with new business. Not to forgive is to yield oneself to another's control... to be locked into a sequence of act and response, of outrage and revenge, tit for tat, escalating always. The present is endlessly overwhelmed and devoured by the past. Forgiveness frees the forgiver. It extracts the forgiver from someone else's nightmare." - Lance Morrow

It has been observed, that "resentment is a form of hurt ego. It is an outgrowth of self-pity. A rebellion against events or people who have thrust at one's pride, interests, ambitions. One who is given to resentment feels that he has been frustrated by an act or event. The way to overcome resentment is to step outside of self."[19] Charles Allen, the great integrator of psychiatry and theology, says there four problems that are foremost in humanity - fear, guilt, self-centeredness and the inability to forgive. He says it is the last one – the inability to forgive - is the hardest to deal with.[20]

To forgive is to commit the matter to God. If the other person is wrong, then the Holy Spirit will convict them. They will end up in God's court, under discipline. They will end up in lock-down, in an emotional prison. God does pursue the guilty. But, he wants us to be agents of release. As we have been forgiven, so should we forgive. Freely we have received, freely we should give.

Finally, the plea of the prayer is for spiritual protection from the Evil One. We are not only to pray for our deliverance, but for the hand of God to be on others as they navigate the maze of daily life. "Let them not come into the hand of the Evil One!" Deliver them. This is a prayer for spiritual insight, for wisdom in decisions, for spiritual guidance.

Pray the prayer:

> *God, you are Father, our Father, my Father, my King and the architect of my life. You have a plan for me – and I ask today that you direct my steps according to your will. You are my provider, for all my needs today. You are my ultimate Judge. I don't want to end up in your courtroom – please, forgive me and may I be a forgiving person. You are a warrior God, the protector of my life. Keep me from sin. Deliver me from the Evil One. Let me live a life of triumph. Let my life glorify you. Reveal through me your power and your glory. Amen.*

In "The Man of La Mancha" the lead character sings the wonderful song, "To Dream the Impossible Dream." He meets Aldonza. Though she is a prostitute, he calls her, "My lady!" And then he declares, "I give you a new name – Dulcinea." He sees her not as she is, but as she can be. It is too much for her. She screams, "Don't call me a Lady. I was born in a ditch by a mother who left me there, naked and cold and too hungry to cry. I never blamed her. I'm sure she left hoping that I'd have the good sense to die. Look at me. I'm no lady. I'm only a kitchen slut, reeking with sweat. A strumpet men use and forget. Don't call me Dulcinea. I am only Aldonza and I am nothing at all!"

Overwhelmed with shame and polluted by guilt, without hope or dignity, Aldonza disappears into the darkness. But the Man of La Mancha is relentless as she withdraws, he objects, "But you are my lady, Dulcinea." Here is the gospel. It is Christ who has come to the earth, searching and calling for His Bride, the Church. It is Hosea calling out to Gomer. It is God calling to Israel. "But you are my child. You're a child of God. He loves you, even if you are a lost soul. Find and follow the faith God has for you. You'll be born again and turned into a beautiful, 'blessing to be a blessing' soul."

In the last act of the play, the knight is dying. He has been condemned as an outcast. He is considered a crazy person. His impossible dream is in peril. His heart is broken. And to his dying bed comes a lady. She's beautiful. She is dressed in mantilla and lace. A heavenly choir sings in the background. She prays. He opens his eyes. "Who are you?" he asks. She rises. She stands erect. She answers, "My name? My name is Dulcinea." Aldonza has been born again. She has been transformed. The unbeliever has become a believer. The sinner has become a saint. The impossible has happened. How could such a change take place? It is simple, and yet, profound. She came to believe what the knight believed about her. What the Man of La Mancha believed she could and would become. "I am not what I think I am. I am not what you think I am. I am what I think you think I am." It is only when we get into our head, what Christ has in his head, about us, that transformation takes place.[21] I am what God thinks about me!

> *To dream ... the impossible dream ...*
> *To fight ... the unbeatable foe ...*
> *To bear ... with unbearable sorrow ...*
> *To run ... where the brave dare not go ...*
> *To right ... the unrightable wrong ...*
> *To love ... pure and chaste from afar ...*
> *To try ... when your arms are too weary ...*
> *To reach ... the unreachable star ...*

This is my quest, to follow that star ...
No matter how hopeless, no matter how far ...
To fight for the right, without question or pause ...
To be willing to march into Hell, for a Heavenly cause ...

And I know if I'll only be true, to this glorious quest,
That my heart will lie will lie peaceful and calm, when I'm laid to my rest ...
And the world will be better for this:
That one man, scorned and covered with scars,
Still strove, with his last ounce of courage,
To reach ... the unreachable star ...[22]

Prayer, time with God, alters our perspective!

Principle Four
Prayer Demands Persistence

*Prayer must be aflame.
Its ardor must consume.
Prayer without fervor is as a sun
without light or heat, or as a flower
without beauty or fragrance.
A soul devoted to God is a fervent soul,
and prayer is the creature of that flame.
He only can truly pray who is all aglow
for holiness, for God, and for heaven.*

E. M. Bounds

4

Malcolm Muggeridge concluded that the most stunning political fact of the last century was the inability of the USSR, with every means of suppression at its disposal, to destroy the Church within its borders. With only state approved and registered churches open, churches that agreed to comply with state standards, many Christians joined an underground movement.

Years before, the Jews of the exile whose faith had been defined by a temple, a place with its priesthood and ceremonies, learned to adapt. So these Christians learned that faith was not a matter of place, but a relationship with the person, Jesus Christ. Suddenly, personal prayer became a defining feature of their lives. Without public and open faith gatherings, private moments with God came to be cherished. Without abundant Bibles, scrapes of Scripture verses were passed between Christians and hidden in their hearts. When the revolution came, missionaries fled. Churches were closed. Christians were openly persecuted. The treatment of any other group with such disdain would have led to an international human rights crisis. Despite all the persecution and oppression, the church survived. Now the church is more resilient than ever before. It is indestructible. It is the extension of Christ himself.[23]

When George Bush was Vice President of the United States, he attended the funeral of former Soviet boss Leonid Brezhnev. At the end of the ceremony, the widow of Brezhnev stood motionless by the casket of her husband, as if she were in another world. No one could have guessed the moment of conscience she was having. Then, just before the coffin lid was closed, the widow of Brezhnev did a bold and daring thing for that era of the most dominant Communist nation on the face of the earth. As the soldiers reached to touch and close the coffin lid, the widow of the powerful communist leader reached inside the coffin, and drew the sign of the cross over her husband's chest.

In the global stronghold of cold atheistic power, the woman who had stood at the side of one of the most powerful and godless leaders of his time in human history, expressed hope in the cross of Christ. It was an act of civil disobedience. It was an act of bold faith. It was a declaration of dissonance. With the world watching, she boldly stood with and simultaneously against her husband. It was an act of love, and of hope. It was an act of courageous differentiation. One wonders about the private conversations that might have taken place which preceded such a moment. There it was, in front of the whole world, in the face of global dignitaries, in the shadow of the Kremlin,

> *If your faith does not make you pray, have nothing to do with it: get rid of it, and God help thee to begin again.*
> — C. H. Spurgeon

with Party bosses standing nearby, proof of enduring faith under a roof shared with the Soviet Boss, himself. A grieving widow reached out to a loving God. George Bush said he was deeply moved by her silent protest.[24]

It does not take communism to create similar suppression. I write this note watching various thanksgiving festivities on American television – in free America. The root of the holiday is about gratitude to God – the God of the Bible. But no one, not one commentator, not one guest, will dare mention the One to whom we should be grateful.

There is much talk about "what" we are thankful for – family and friends. But no one mentions the "Who" to whom we should be thankful. The repression is so strong, the social conformity so deeply enforced, not by political might, but by mere psychological force, and by collective intimidation, that no one dares cross the line, not even in subtle ways. Here, the political influencers, with the help of the courts and various private and public educational institutions, have accomplished virtually the same end as did atheistic communism. In truth, ours is the more terrible form of atheism. It is not the militant and passionate struggle against the idea of God himself, but in the practical atheism of everyday living, indifference and languor, inactivity and indolence. Sadly, we encounter these forms of atheism among those who are formally Christians. God has been banished from the public square, and no one has protested. We lack persistence! We are conformist – to the culture.

There was a core of believers in the USSR that refused to conform. They defied the edicts. They worshipped and served the only true and living God. They risked their lives to keep the underground church alive. In 1988, Moscow marked the 70th anniversary of the Bolshevik revolution. As the date neared, Christians in the underground Church began to plead for global intercessors to join them in prayer. A number of worldwide Christian agencies set January of that year as a month of prayer. No one knew what, if anything would happen. But faith believed that the 70th year had significance.

> *The story of every great Christian achievement is in the history of answered prayer.*
> *E. M. Bounds*

In the underground church, the mantra had become. "Seventy years is long enough!" Persistent prayer intensified. No one knew what would result. On the first working day, after that month of prayer by Christians around the world, Premier Michel Gorbachev did something that was stunning. He released all religious prisoners across the U.S.S.R. It was unthinkable. In one stroke, seventy years of persecution and oppression ended. It was breathtaking. Atheistic communism had begun its melt-down. Campus Crusade for Christ immediately translated the JESUS FILM into the Russian language. When the film premiered in Moscow, the Secretary of Education requested copies for Russian public schools. The Academy of Sciences and government departments did the same for their personnel. Mission agencies united under the banner of Co-Mission and for the next five years, they trained 38,000 public school teachers in the former Soviet Republics to teach ethics and morality in what had previously been Communist classrooms. Some 60 percent of the public school teachers throughout the nation trusted Christ as Savior.[25] Persistent prayer paid off. Persistent prayer may have toppled a government.

Similar things have happened here within our boundaries. Two-hundred years ago, Supreme Court Justice John Marshall suggested that "the church is too far gone ever to be redeemed." The few Christians on college campuses convened in secret to avoid persecution. The epidemic of alcoholism - 300,000 drunks in a population of 5,000,000 - plagued America. With the moral slump at its worst in 1794, churches of nearly all denominations rallied to a call for united agreement in prayer. Revival in the churches and moral recovery in the young nation followed. Could that happen again? Not without persistence in prayer!

When Jesus taught on prayer he emphasized persistence. In Luke 18 we read:

> *And he spake a parable unto them to this end, that men ought always to pray, and not to faint (Luke 18:1).*

The purpose of this parable was to encourage prayer – always. Prayer is a constant. It is an on-going facet of our life in God. There is no spiritual life without prayer, only the simulation of it, only a fake spiritual life, an illusion. Jesus urged men to pray and not to faint or not to give up. It is like breathing. E. M. Bounds urged, "Four things let us keep in mind: God hears prayer, God heeds prayer, God answers prayer. And God delivers by prayer."

> *Neglected prayer is the birthplace of all evil.*
> —Spurgeon

Such prayer demands discipline. And discipline is no problem for a disciplined disciple. It is a problem for cultural Christians, whose faith is largely superficial "jesus-talk." Read and study the lives of every great Christian in history, look at the details of their daily schedules, and you will discover a common thread. No saint has ever adorned the church with the beauty of their sanctified life, without displaying the great characteristic of discipline and order. Invariably, discipline, true discipleship, is the universal characteristic of all the outstanding men and women of God. Someone has said, "Men do not decide their future. They decide their habits and their habits decide their future." There are three disciplines in Matthew 6 and they anchor the follower of Jesus Christ.

The three are – giving, prayer and fasting. Giving is my relationship to all things external. If you cannot give it away, you do not own it. It owns you. And giving is related to prayer. Grasping hearts evidences selfishness in prayer, a clear obstacle to answers.

Prayer is my relationship to time and all things eternal. If I do not value time with God here and now, it is a signal of where my heart is. It is either here in the now, or there in eternity; here consumed with the earth, or there in heaven. The one thing that keeps working after I die, is the effect of my prayer life. If a Christian does not have time to pray, time to spend alone with God, his life is out of control. He has no discipline over his schedule. He is a slave to the world's system. It is laughable. God wants an appointment with him, daily. But, he has no time for God. God may choose to ride with him on an errand, or talk with him as he takes his daily shower or does some chore. But God will have to run along beside him and talk as he, the important human, busies himself with his daily duties. This is life upside down. He is rushing headlong into eternity, evidencing no time to regularly meet God.

Finally, fasting controls all things internal. Hunger is the greatest drive of the body. Subduing the flesh is paramount for spirit-controlled living. Fasting is the sign that spiritual hunger has triumphed over fleshly hunger.

Here are the keys to control – over time and eternity, prayer; - over the flesh and all internal drives, fasting; - over all things external, giving. For each of these disciplines there is a promised reward. Persistence in prayer is impossible without discipline. Such ideas are commonly viewed today as legalism.

> "It is wrong to say that we are being 'legalistic' when we are concerned with the ordering of our Christian life and with our faithfulness in requirements of scripture reading and prayer. Disorder undermines and destroys the faith."[26]

The Message of Luke 18: Don't Give Up On Prayer

It is interesting that the concern of Jesus was that we might give up on prayer. In fact, prayer is the first thing we tend to give up on. We give up on prayer before we give up on Church attendance or preaching, teaching, or other activities. To emphasize persistence in prayer, Jesus tells this interesting story.

> *There was in a city a judge, which feared not God, neither regarded man: And there was a widow in that city; and she came unto him, saying, Avenge me of mine adversary. And he would not for a while:*

but afterward he said within himself, Though I fear not God, nor regard man; Yet because this widow troubleth me, I will avenge her, lest by her continual coming she weary me. Luke 18:2-5.

This is one of those stories that move us to "protect" God. It makes Him appear harsh and insensitive. We must storm heaven and bang the door down in order to move Him to answer and even then it seems that he could care less about us. Spurgeon said, "Pray until you can pray. For it is when you think you cannot pray that is when you are praying."

The Meaning of the Parable: Contrast – Not Comparison
But this parable is not about comparison. It is about contrast. Notice the differences.

The Judge is...	God is ..
Insensitive	Sensitive
Cold and Hard	Warm and Caring
Inconsiderate	Considerate
Unjust	Very Just – even merciful and Gracious
Appears biased	Fair
Without respect of men	Loving toward men
Willing to allow the widow hurt	Not willing that any perish

This man should not have been a judge. And this woman could not have handpicked a worse scenario than to end up in the jurisdiction of this particular judge. Here again is contrast. In that culture, to be a woman meant that you were disadvantaged socially. But to be a widow was a double disadvantage. A widow who had been married was not as desirable as an unmarried virgin. Without a husband, there may have been no man to be her social protector or advocate. That seems clear from our text. She has an adversary from which she herself cannot get relief. So she turns to justice and asks for relief. But she gets no justice. It is not mercy she seeks. Only justice. But there is no social system to protect women as we see in this courtroom. Her response is vigilant persistence. She will not give up. She will not be intimidated. She will not be told "No!"

It is here that another contrast is clear between this woman and us:

The woman is ...	And we ...
Determined	Are undetermined
Tireless in persistence	Tire easily of persistent prayer
Refuses to give up	Faint
Continual and consistent	Are sporadic and inconsistent

E. M. Bounds called a prayerless ministry "the undertaker" for God's church. He claimed that "a prayerless Christian will never learn God's truth" – is Spiritual discerned. The Bible is understood when it is read by a man on his knees. And, Bounds said, "a prayerless ministry will never be able to teach God's truth." The truths of God need supernatural energy which comes only by prayer to penetrate darkened hearts. "Ages of millennial glory have been lost by prayerless church. The coming of our Lord has been postponed indefinitely by prayerless church. Hell has enlarged herself

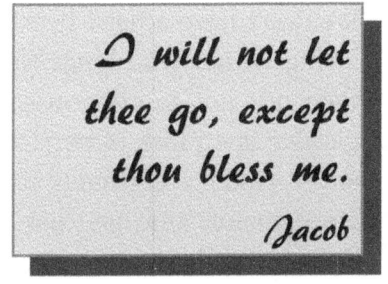

> *I will not let thee go, except thou bless me.*
> — Jacob

and filled her dire caves in the presence of the dead service of the prayerless church."[27]

The Bottom-Line: God Answers Persistent Prayer
Listen to Jesus again:

And the Lord said, Hear what the unjust judge saith.

Shall not God avenge his own elect, which cry day and night unto him, though he bear long with them?

I tell you that he will avenge them speedily. Nevertheless when the Son of man cometh, shall he find faith on the earth? Luke 18:6-8.

The point of the parable is that if a socially disadvantaged widow can move a hard-hearted, insensitive judge by her persistent request, how much more will the prayers of God's people touch Him?

We don't have a hard-hearted judge in heaven. We have a loving Father who longs to hear and answer prayer. Why then are not more prayers answered? The point of the parable is - a lack of persistence. We give up in prayer too easily. God has chosen to use prayer as a character builder! He demands that we "ask and keep-on asking; seek and keep-on seeking; knock and keep-on knocking." Prayer strengthens persistence and determination.

Bill Hybels says that God always answers prayer, and that sometimes he says, "No!" When our request are wrong, unwise for us, or out of Scriptural bounds, God loves us enough to say, "No!" in answer to our request. At other times, God says, "Grow!" The problem may not be in the request itself. It is rather that God sees something in us as more important than the answer to our prayer. So He subordinates our prayer request to our growth in grace. "Grow! He bids us." Then there are times when God says, "Slow!" The request is right. And we are right before him, but the timing is wrong. So God calls us to patience. Then there are those wonderful times when the request is right, we are right, the timing is right – and in such moments Hybels quotes God as saying, "Go!"

God always answers prayer – "No; Grow; Slow or Go!"

In the end, Jesus asked, "When the Son of man comes will he find faith on the earth?" He has not changed subjects. He is reminding us that if persistent prayer has endured, then faith will be alive on the earth. Here is his point – the survival of faith in the earth rises or falls on our persistence in prayer. Without prayer, vibrant faith ceases. Another form of faith may survive, but it will be a twisted and distorted version of New Testament faith. That demands prayer.

> "God's most exquisite gift to man - the crown jewel of His gifts, is the ability to converse with him in prayer."[28]

Thorlief Holmglad was a pastor in Oslo a century ago. Those were dismal years for Norway. As the pastor stepped from his pulpit, his excited custodian saw the look of despair on his face, "There's going to be a revival in this church!" he said to the pastor. The pastor turned and faced the empty pews, "Revival? Does this look like revival?" Come with me, the custodian said, leading the pastor to a spot behind the pulpit. "Do you see those water marks on the carpet? Those are tear stains. I have been praying and weeping here for five years. The lord has assured me he is going to send a revival!"

The custodian was not alone. In a nearby city, two sisters were crying out to God for revival. Their burden for renewal had become heavy. "If it is your will for us to continue to pray, then send other intercessors." The two became four. The four became eight. The eight became sixteen. These small pockets of believers persisted in prayer for revival, and against all odds. And yet the revival did not begin in the home of the intercessors, nor yet behind the pulpit where the custodian had prayed.

> *Satan trembles when he sees, The weakest saint upon his knees.*

It happened in the most unlikely place. In a Sunday evening youth meeting, filled with restless, disinterested youngsters, a cloud of God's glory appeared visibly to the youth leader. As he struggled to gain the attention of the young people, the white cloud slowly descended from the ceiling. To his dismay and disbelief, the more the presence of the cloud filled the room, the more restless the young people became. Finally, it touched the tops of their heads. Instantly, young people fell to their knees praying, weeping, confessing their sins. The tenor of that youth meeting impacted the adult evening worship service. Adults were themselves weeping and repenting of sin in prayer. Special services were conducted the next evening on Monday. Then on Tuesday. They continued throughout the week. A spirit of brokenness persisted and the revival continued for twelve years. It spread to other churches. Then to other cities and finally to the nation. Some 20,000 people were converted and added to Christ in the city of Olso alone.[29]

Roger Simms was just returning home from military duty and was hitchhiking. To his surprise a shiny new black car stopped to pick him up. He carefully loaded his heavy duffle bag and got in the passenger seat where he was greeted by the friendly smile of the driver, a sharp looking older gentleman.

> "Hello, son. Are you on leave or are you going home for good?"
>
> "I just got out of the army, and I'm going home for the first time in a long, long time," answered Roger.
>
> "Well, if you are going to Chicago, you are in luck," smiled the man.
>
> "I'm not going as far as Chicago, but my home is right on the way to Chicago, so I guess this is my lucky day. Thank you. My name is Roger Simms."
>
> "Mr. Simms, I'm Mr. Hanover."
>
> "Nice to meet you sir. Do you live in Chicago?"
>
> "Yes. I live there and have a business there."

They continued to exchange stories. As they got closer to Roger's home, Roger, who was a Christian felt impressed that he should broach the subject of faith. "Mr. Hanover, have you ever heard of the difference between religion and Christianity?"

"I was always under the impression Christianity was a religion," replied Hanover.

"Not really, said Roger. You see Religion is always spelled '*DO*'. Everyone into religion is always trying to do something to please God and be acceptable. The only problem is nobody can know for sure if they've done enough. In fact the bible tells us, we can't do enough to be acceptable. Where religion is spelled '*DO*,' Christianity is spelled '*DONE*'. On the cross, Christ finished everything for us. He did everything for us to be acceptable to God. He even shouted from the cross, 'It is finished!' Which could be translated 'paid in full.' He paid the penalty for our sin. All we need to do is receive the gift he has given us. Mr. Hanover, it isn't enough to know this, the Bible says we have to receive it. '*Yet to all who received him, to those who believed in his name, he gave the right to become children of God*' *(John 1:12)*. Mr. Hanover, would you like to receive Christ as your Savior?"

Even as Roger framed the question he realized, Mr. Hanover was pulling his big car off the shoulder of the road and coming to a stop. *Here it is*, Roger thought, *he's going to ask me to get out.* But he didn't. Mr. Hanover didn't even look at Roger. He bowed his head and quietly began to weep. After a moment, Roger asked again, "Mr. Hanover, would you like to ask Christ into your life?"

Mr. Hanover nodded an affirmation, then said, "What do I say?"

Roger led Mr. Hanover in a simple prayer asking for

forgiveness for sins, and asking Christ to be Savior, and thanking Him for what he did for him on the cross.

"Thank you for talking to me about this Roger. What you said is exactly what I needed to hear. I thought I would never be able to be a Christian. I thought somehow I needed to change everything. Now I understand it isn't up to me, but Christ. This is the best thing that ever happened to me."

After some more talking, Mr. Hanover drove to Roger's house, gave him his business card thanked him again and dropped him off.

But that's not the end of the story. Five years went by. Roger got married and had a child. One day, while he was packing for a business trip to Chicago, he found the business card that Mr. Hanover had given him five years before. He decided that while he was in Chicago he would try to look him up.

In Chicago, Roger looked up Hanover Enterprises. The building was impressive. When he asked the receptionist if he could see Mr. Hanover, she replied that would be impossible. He tried to let her know that they were old friends.

"If you are old friends, then you can see Mrs. Hanover," she replied.

A little disappointed, Roger was led to an office down the hall. A woman in her fifties was sitting behind a huge oak desk. She extended her hand, "You knew my husband?"

Five Basic Prayer Principles

Roger explained how he had met Mr. Hanover about five years ago, when he was so kind as to give him a ride home after his military service had ended.

A strange look came over Mrs. Hanover's face, and she asked, "Would you be able to tell me what date it was, by any chance, when Mr. Hanover gave you a ride?"

Thinking it a strange question, Roger answered nonetheless, because he knew precisely the day of his discharge, and said so. "It was May 7th the day of my discharge, mam."

Mrs. Hanover seemed even more peculiar. "Did anything special happen on your ride? I mean did anything unusual take place?" She asked.

Roger hesitated, unsure whether this woman would now be angry at him over what had taken place. Was she an atheist who was angry at her husband's change? Had this been a source of contention between them? For a moment, he was tempted withhold the details of the private prayer time. But again, he felt impressed to tell what happened. "Yes Mrs. Hanover, something very special happened that day. Your husband accepted the Lord Jesus as his savior. I explained to him the gospel, and he pulled over and wept and asked Jesus to come into his life. He was very happy about it."

Suddenly, Mrs. Hanover began to weep uncontrollably. *What was going on here?* Roger could hardly guess. He simply put his hand on her shoulder and let her regain her composure. She was finally able to explain her behavior.

> "I grew up in a Christian home. My husband did not. I was warned not to marry a non-believer, but I loved

him. I prayed for him all these years. I was sure God would bring him around. On May 7th I thought God had failed me. He didn't answer my prayers. Mr. Hanover was killed on May 7th in a horrible head on collision. He never arrived home. I haven't been the same since. I stopped trusting God. How could God allow this to happen? How could God take him away and not answer all those prayers? I've been blaming God for these last 5 years."

Persistent prayer pays off – even when we fail to see the results. Mr. Hanover died a believer. And Mrs. Hanover recovered her faith. Never give up on God or the promises he has made, and the people we have entrusted to him in believing prayer.

Principle Five
**Powerful Things
Happen With Prayer**

*There is nothing the devil dreads so much
as prayer?
The Kneeling Christian*

*There is a marked absence of travail.
There is much phrasing, but little
pleading.
Prayer has become a soliloquy instead
of a passion. The powerlessness of the
church needs no other explanation ...*

*To be prayerless is to be
both passionless and powerless.
They who prevail in the secret place of the
Most High cannot be beaten anywhere.
Samuel Chadwick*

5

T. W. Hunt, the great Baptist leader said, "Prayerlessness is a statement to God that we do not believe that spiritual forces have the power to affect a world created by a spiritual being."[30] This is what the godless believe - that the real power is in the visible, the seen, the measurable dimension. It is pointless to pray "for Kings and all who are in authority" if we do not believe that our prayers affect thrones.

In the archives of press releases from the days of World War II comes the following:

> Twelve boys, who met every Sunday for three years after the fall of Bataan to pray for divine guidance for the Allied leaders, today had the personal thanks of an American General. The boys - too young to fight -decided 10 days after the fall of Bataan that they would do something to help victory. They decided it would be prayer. Major General Edward P. King, the man who was forced to surrender Bataan and then make the death march, visited the boys yesterday. He was back from more than two years in a Japanese prison camp. He said he wanted to thank the 13-

to-14 year-old youngsters personally. He told them that faith means more than anything else to soldiers facing death. 'Men who do not expect to live become very close to God', King said. 'Men who avoid the chaplain most during peacetime will walk ten miles for one when he expects to die." King said he wished the men on Bataan had known about the Atlanta prayer band. He said he was certain that their weekly prayers had been a mighty influence.

The boys prayed - and wrote letters. They prayed for Allied leaders regularly and sent prayer support letters. As they listened to Major General King, their faces glowed. Their bold prayer band had already received letters of thanks from General MacArthur, Admiral Nimitz, Field Marshal Montgomery, Winston Churchill and President Roosevelt. The boys started their weekly prayer effort with one name on their prayer list. Before they finished their three year prayer vigil, they had 150 names on their list. Every Sunday they would repeat every one of the names with bowed heads and reverent hearts. It had been the words of General MacArthur that

> *We think of prayer as a preparation for work, or a calm after having done work whereas prayer is the essential work. It is the supreme activity of everything that is noblest in our personality.*
> Oswald Chambers

had led the boys to form the group. "With divine guidance," MacArthur had said, "We cannot fail." That was when the boys decided that prayer was mightier than the forces of war. Admiral Nimitz wrote in August, 1942, "The prayers of these boys for ultimate victory will be answered." Roosevelt sent a picture weeks before his death with the inscription, "To the boys of the Bataan prayer band. From their friend."[31]

Nothing is clearer in the New Testament than the connection between prayer and spiritual power. Armin Gesswein observed in his book, *Everything by Prayer*, that "Pentecost did not come through a preaching service; Pentecost came to a prayer service. From Pentecost to Patmos, God never departs from the pattern."

E. M. Bounds says, "God's Word is a record of prayer - of praying men and their achievements, of the divine warrant of prayer and of the encouragement given to those who pray." Bounds says, " The success of His work in this world, is committed to prayer ... praying men have been God's vice regents on earth ..."[32] The book of Acts is a book about a praying church. Notice the connection between prayer and the great break-through moments in the history of the early church.

Prayer Invites the Holy Spirit
In Acts 2, a prayer meeting matures on the Day of Pentecost. Into that prayer meeting descends the Spirit. The whole building appears to be on fire. The sound of a heavenly storm fills the room, loud enough to be heard across the city. It is the roar of the slain lamb, the Lion of the Tribe of Judah. He is back, by the Spirit, to empower his church. Tongues of fire dance on each of the heads of the 120 newborn, Spirit-filled saints. For the first time since Babel, the whole earth

is linguistically united. Everyone hears the message in their own tongue. At the end of the day, 3,000 souls are reaped and the New Testament church is launched.

Prayer Releases Healing Power
In Acts 3, it is to a prayer meeting that Peter and John are headed. It is near the hour of 3:00 p.m., the time the evening sacrifice would be prepared and offered at the Temple. It will be across Jerusalem and the Jewish world, an hour of prayer. Entering the Temple compound at the Gate Beautiful, the pair of Spirit-filled apostles encountered a lame man begging alms. Peter is both compassionate and penniless, but he is not poor. "Silver and Gold have I none, but such as I have give I thee. In the name of Jesus rise and walk."

Immediately, the Bible says, his ankles received strength and the lame man rose and walked. It was one more frustration for the Jewish leaders – their Passover had been affected by a siege of darkness and an earthquake that rent the precious and sacred veil between the holy place and the most holy place into two pieces, and it was at this same hour of prayer, fifty days earlier. All they could do was sew it back together. Their feast of the first-fruits had been overshadowed by the resurrection rumors that encircled the city, three days later. Their Feast of Pentecost had also been interrupted by the 120 and the thousands who came to believe that Jesus was not dead, but alive. Now, there is yet this, another disturbance, a lame man healed in the name of Jesus. They can't get rid of Jesus. He keeps popping up everywhere. Crucify Him and he rises from the dead, and then multiplies himself. First, there are 120 of Him. Then 3000. Soon, the number will embrace 5000 households, ten-to-twenty percent of the entire population of the city.

Prayer Shakes Sacred Space and Emboldens the Church

The threats are intensified and the pressure sends the faithful to their knees. They gather for prayer. And into that prayer meeting, recorded in Acts 4, the power of God comes in such force that "the place where they were assembled was shaken." The supernatural character of the death and resurrection of Christ is objectified so many times – the darkness in the ninth hour, at the time of his death, the rent veil, the stone rolled away, the linen shroud left like a caterpillar when the butterfly crawls out of his cocoon, the napkin neatly folded, the multiple appearances of Christ, the ascension, the coming of the Spirit with objective signs: audible wind (a sound), visible fire (sight), empowerment and supernatural speech (tongues), fire on each of their heads (the personal attachment of the Spirit). The healing of the lame man (Acts 3), and now, the place, the physical space around them is vibrating. And there is the effect, the extraordinary change in the disciples – boldness, articulate abilities previously unknown, persuasive skills. They had changed. They had power and capacities they did not previously possess.

Prayer Renews Church Growth and Unifies

In Acts 6, the effect of the growth of the church is now staggering. Their care for the poor and the disadvantaged is a major portion of their work. Despite all their efforts, the Greeks among them feel that they are being slighted. For the first time, ethnic differences allow the suggestion of prejudice. It is a stunning charge. Are they not one? Have they not been forged together through the blood of Christ into a new man, a transcendent identity?

The apostles recognize suddenly that they have allowed an imbalance to occur in their own lives. They have been drawn into the overwhelming work of public ministry, at the expense of the priority of private time with God. Their personal growth, and the spiritual and relational health of the Church itself, and that of the people, demands a deeper root system than they are nurturing in private times with God. The diagnosis is so foreign to us. That the health of the church, that the quality of relationships in the church, is somehow tied to the prayer life of the leaders – what an idea!

They make a wise decision. They will appoint men to carry on supporting ministries. And to those men will be committed the ministry to the disadvantaged. The men are to be wise and filled with the Spirit, mature, and they are also chosen to reflect diversity in ethnic leadership. The apostles, will recommit themselves to prayer and the word. Here is their recognition that church affairs and business have wrongly ordered the apostolic calling. They were called to prayer and the word, not to tables. When the balance is restored, the Church again sees growth and division is healed.

Rabbi Liebman died the young age of 41, only three years after the release of his immensely popular book, *Peace of Mind*. What an irony! After the release of that popular book, Charles Allen writes, "He was swamped with people seeking peace. His mail was heavy, his telephone rang constantly, people came to him steadily all day and even to his home at night. He was a kind-hearted man ..."[33] Evidently, he could not turn them away. In the end, he lost the peace, the *shalom*, that he himself had discovered and written about. So it is, when we completely give ourselves to others, no matter how noble our intent, and we have little or no time left for God, we end up having nothing to give to people.

Prayer Delivers

Herod, the grandson of Herod the Great that ruled during time Jesus was born, wanted to retain the favor of the Jewish people and their leaders. While he had little hope of having them like him, or even to respect him, he knew certain favors would curry peace. And Herod wanted peace in his province.

In Jerusalem, He even observed certain aspects of Judaism, acting publicly as if he were an observant Jew. In his short reign of three years (A.D. 41-4), his means of countermanding Jewish distaste for foreign rule and for his Roman background, not to mention his Edomite ancestry, was his observance of Jewish customs and public support of the Jewish faith.[34]

It was, however, all an act. Noticing Christians as a dissident sect within Judaism, a source of social and religious dissension, and believing them to be no more than that, he made a fatal decision. He saw the opportunity to gain Jewish favor, particularly with the leaders, by executing the prominent members of the 'heretical Christian sect.' That action, he evidently believed, should convince Jewish leaders of his sensitivity to their will. Perhaps, they would be more favorably disposed toward him. If not, he would have another bargaining chip on his side of the table.

So in Acts 12, the church is under another siege of persecution. James, the brother of John, and a prominent apostle, has been martyred. By beheading James, Herod was making a gesture of solidarity with the Jewish majority. It was a public relations ploy to demonstrate his loyalty to Judaism. The Feast of Unleavened Bread was just beginning when Peter was arrested (12:3). The seven-day period was inclusive of the Passover (12:4). Peter was to remain in jail until the festival cycle was completed. Then, Herod evidently was intent on placing Peter on trial and executing him as he had James. He preferred to wait until the festival was over. As in the time of Jesus, the Jewish leaders constituted a small minority and their opinion did not always represent that of the general population. Another public execution during a sacred season could cause repercussions. Remember, the chief priests had sought to avoid the execution of Jesus during the festival of Unleavened Bread fearing a public riot (Mark 14:2).

So Peter was held in prison during the Feast of Unleavened Bread and the Passover. The whole story represents an irony. Peter, a Jew, was imprisoned on the Passover, the great, cheerful day of liberty from the shackles of slavery. He was confined, not free. The Jewish people, delivered from slavery, were now making prisoners of their own brothers during the season of liberation. Luke seems intent on pointing out the irony.[35] Yet, Peter was not fretting. He was sleeping soundly! Tomorrow, he might die, but tonight, he would sleep like a baby. Herod had taken every precaution to make sure that Peter did not escape. He had probably been informed, that Peter was once before placed in custody, only to be found free, without an explanation (5:19-24). The location of Peter was probably the Antonia Fortress, a military barracks that later housed Paul for a brief period (21:31-23:32). That fortress complex was conjoined to and overlooked the temple. Peter was such an important prisoner, he was guarded by four squads of four soldiers each, probably on a rotating basis. He had never had so much attention. Luke notes that Peter was sleeping peacefully on the eve of his trial and execution (12:6). He had faith that his life was safe in Christ.

Powerful Things Happen with Prayer

The Church gathered for prayer. And God sent an angel to Peter. Acts 12:6 says the apostle "was sleeping between two soldiers, bound with two chains, and sentries (plural) stood guard at the entrance out of the prison." Suddenly, the cell was filled with light. The angel manifested to Peter, struck him on the side to awaken him. "Quick, get up!" he said, and the chains fell off Peter's wrists. The angel again struck him on the side and said to him, *"Put on your clothes and sandals ... Wrap your cloak around you and follow me"* (Acts 12:8-9). Peter does so, but apparently stunned. Suddenly, the remainder of his chains fell off – here again is the power of God objectified. Peter followed the angel through very real bars and physical objects. For these brief moments, Peter's physical body is endowed with powers that transcend the natural. At first, Peter must have thought he was having a dream or vision. The Scripture says, *"They passed the first and second guards and came to the iron gate leading to the city."* Not only is he endowed with power to defy natural obstacles, but he is endowed with invisibility. To some, this is beyond belief. But there is more.

> *Do the angels veil their faces before You, and shall I be content to prattle through a form with no soul and no heart?*
> C. H. Spurgeon

Standing before the gate, a very real physical obstruction, the gate *"opened for them by itself, and they went through it"* (12:9-10). Together, the angel and Peter walked the length of one street, and suddenly the angel left him, he was gone. It was at this moment, that Peter *"came to himself"* (12:11). He

85

would say to himself at that moment, *"Now I know without a doubt that the Lord sent his angel and rescued me from Herod's clutches and from everything the Jewish people were anticipating"* (12:11). Here is the clear indication that the Jewish authorities were anticipating Herod's execution of Peter. But it was not to be. Another power was at work, one different than the angelic intervention and yet in the mystery of God's ways, one that was simultaneously conjoined.

Now free, Peter headed for the home of Mary, the mother of Mark (12:12). The absence of the mention of her husband is a clue that she was a widow. Her home was a place where believers gathered, and that night they had come together for a prayer meeting.

All that King Herod could do could not bind Peter. His life was not in the hands of that King. He was not subject to the clutches of iron shackles or hardened soldiers. He escaped, in spite of Herod's determined intent to keep him securely in stocks. The contrast is striking – Herod has no power, God is in charge.

The church was praying – and God answered. There is power in prayer. An angel released Peter from prison, but prayer fetched the angel. When Peter reached the gate at the home of Mary, an indication that she did not live in a simple home, he was met by the only gate or door that he could not freely pass through – another irony. Rhoda, Mary's household servant, answered the door. The church was still on their knees, praying. Rhoda, also a believer, was joyfully shocked to see Peter, so surprised that she left him outside, without opening the door for him.

Inside, she attempted to convey the message that the prayers of the group had been heard – Peter was not only free, he was at the door. Here we meet another contradiction. The very sincere believers who were earnestly praying that God would intervene and spare Peter could not believe Rhoda's report. "You're out of your mind," they told her. When she kept insisting that it was so, they said, "It must be his angel." Beyond prayer and faith, mixed with angelic intervention and the temporary endowment to Peter of transcendent abilities, is the sovereignty of God. Prayer, in one sense, has no power. God has the power. But it is prayer that seems so often to link supernatural intervention on earth with sovereign action from heaven. God works his purposes in ways that are beyond our understanding.

The whole story is delightfully disarming. It is far from being some formula for miracles that might be repeated.

1. Peter was confused and stunned by the angelic intervention, even though he had seen it before.
2. Peter delivered, stood at the door, the answer to their prayers, but he couldn't get in. His knocking must have grown more and more intense, as he banged on the door.
3. Rhoda, the servant, without status, saw him and responded. Then she joyfully forgot to open the door for him.
4. The brothers and sisters inside refused to believe the testimony of the servant, Rhoda. Whoever was at the door, could not be Peter, he was in prison. This, even though they have been praying for him.
5. Despite the dismissive attitude, Rhoda, a mere servant, holds her ground. She, the least among them, gets to make the announcement. She, the

servant, probably only a slave, is the first to believe. "You are out of your mind," they chide here. But she is persistent.
6. And with utter astonishment, they finally open the door and let Peter inside.[36]

Peter, after what might have been only a momentary celebration, instructed the group to send word to James, the brother of Jesus, noticeably absent from the prayer meeting, and then Luke records, *"He left for another place"* (12:17). He must have known that Herod would turn the city upside down searching for him. He would not endanger them. Some deliverance is by supernatural intervention. Another part is by common sense. Other apostles may have also left the city for a short season as well. James is left with the task of steering the church through the turbulent season of persecution.

The next morning, there was no small stir about Peter's escape (12:18). The soldiers' who were charged with his custody now faced death. Herod conducted a thorough search and when he could not find Peter, he tortured the guards to see if they had any information and then had them executed (18:19). The Code of Justinian, from a later period, notes that a guard who allows a prisoner to escape was subject to the same penalty the escaped prisoner would have suffered.

God has intervened. Peter has experienced liberation in the Passover season – a liberation connected again to angelic activity and the power of prayer.

Herod and the Jews had experienced a set-back at the hand of the Sovereign God. And God was not finished showing his dominion. Marcus, the governor of Syria and Herod entered in to a dispute of some type that demanded Herod's attention.[37] It evidently involved Tyre and Sidon. An agreement was reached, and the occasion of the new covenant demanded a celebration at which Herod spoke. Luke records, when Herod finished his speech, the audience heralded him as a Divine. "This is the voice of a god, not of a man" (12:22). Herod, a few months prior, had been confronted with the mystery of Peter's release. He must have heard the stories circulating in the streets about the nature of the release. He had seen the fingerprints of God, but he chose to ignore them. Now, he will smitten with a fatal illness for his refusal to acknowledge or "give praise to God" (12:23). Herod, Luke says "was eaten by worms and died" (12:23) a ghastly death.

According to Josephus, Herod was smitten with the strange illness at a festival in honor of Caesar at Caesarea. This festival occurred every five years. Other provincial officials and important dignitaries were in attendance. The date of the festival would have been August 1, A.D. 44, the emperor's birthday, a matter of months after the incident with Peter.[38] On that day, Herod, according to Josephus, donned a silver robe and entered the theater early in the morning, looking resplendent. The flattering mobs, saying he was a god, were not rebuked.[39] Almost immediately after the idolatrous honor, Herod experienced severe cramps. Five days later, he was dead.[40]

Luke, and Josephus, the Jewish historian, both attribute Herod's death to Divine judgment. The three stories – James, Peter and Herod - seem to be purposely strung together in the Scripture to make a point. First, God allows one, James, a significant leader, to die. He thus sends a message to the

Church and to us, that not all will be spared. Following Christ demands a cross. There is a risk involved in being a disciple. Second, he spared Peter in a stunning miracle that defied reason. He did that in answer to prayers prayed by a church that hardly had the faith to believe in the very prayer they were praying. Under the siege of persecution, fresh from the death of James, and facing the loss of Peter, their faith was feeble. But, God still heard their prayer. Third, he turned to the King, to Herod, and he sent his angel to smite Him. One angel delivers. Another judges. Overall, God is sovereign, over the church and the state. And the administration of his sovereignty in the earth is somehow connected to prayer!

At times, he moves miraculously, to protect the church and judge those who oppose his purposes. God will heal the lame man at the temple gate, and then strike Ananias dead. He will deliver Peter from Herod's clutches, and then strike down King Herod himself. With the death of Herod, God puts a stop to his conspiracy with Jewish leaders against the Church. The nature of Herod's death underscores the superficial and hypocritical nature of his Judaism. He was not worshipper of Yahweh. He thought of Himself as a god. The whole affair creates a chilling effect against future persecution of the church, and empowers the faith of the little flock.

Luke says, after the death of Herod, "the word of God continued to increase and spread" (12:24).[41]

Prayer Births Mission
In Acts 13, the Church is gathered in prayer. They are ministering to the Lord. And in that context of worshipful waiting, the Holy Spirit speaks to the Church, "Separate Barnabas and Saul for the work to which I have called

them." It is a significant word, whether by tongues and interpretation or the prophetic, the effect is the same. The church at Antioch is to give birth. They have been blessed with wonderful leaders. Barnabas, such a conciliatory personality, had been sent from Jerusalem. He had retrieved Saul from Tarsus and employed him in a teaching capacity. Five men are mentioned as prophet-teachers. But it is time for the church that has been enjoying such a rich staff, to give them up. They have received, now they must give. Barnabas, who came to them from Jerusalem; and Saul, who came from Tarsus, will be given away to others. The church at Antioch will make it possible for them to "go forth," to "be sent," which is the essence of the apostolic. It is not only the Antioch church that is now called to greater maturity, it is church at large. What will Jerusalem think when it hears that Antioch is sending forth their own apostles? The church as a whole is coming of age.

Into sessions of corporate waiting, of soaking prayer, comes the word of the Lord. It is not born in planning sessions, but in prayer meetings. The church is to be led not by heads, but by hearts. Not by calculating reason, but by the Spirit. Such things seem worlds away from where we are now. Soren Kierkegaard, hardly an evangelical noted, "... Christ did not appoint professors, but followers. If Christianity ... is not reduplicated in the life of the person expounding it, then he does not expound Christianity, for Christianity is a message about living and can only be expounded by being realized in men's lives." It is to be lived, not debated. It is to be experienced, more than it can be explained.

The matter was not simply an inspired utterance and a quick reaction. They tested "the word." They act on the word only after a season of independent and individual "prayer and fasting." What if every call, every missionary couple, every minister or evangelist, church planter or worker was sent only after individual members of the congregation invested personal prayer combined with fasting? What a precious idea this is. First, there is corporate prayer – and a word from the Lord. Then, there is private prayer – with fasting, a search for discernment, a sincere desire to corroborate the message, to find it authentic, but nevertheless, to test it. Such decisions affect lives. Words should be tested when they redirect human destinies. The whole church has a stake in this decision. Here is prayer – and more prayer. Here is spirit-direction, and the greater confirmation of spirit-direction. Only then, does the church lay hands on the two men and send them forth into apostolic ministry. Don't miss the simple point. Apostolic ministry is birthed and confirmed in prayer. The expanding mission of the Church rides on the back of a praying church. Saul is transformed into an apostle – out of a prayer meeting. And Barnabas is commissioned again as one, having first been sent from Jerusalem.

Prayer Rocks the Jailhouse
In Acts 16, Paul and Silas arrive in Philippi. They enquire about believers in the city and hear about "a place of prayer." They arrive at the site of the prayer meeting, down by the river. There, they witness to the women who constitute the prayer meeting. Lydia, a worshipper, but not yet a Christian, opens her heart and home. Following the model of Jesus (Luke 10; Mt. 10), they have found a house of peace and from there they will launch their ministry in the city.

In the midst of their ministry, they have attracted unwanted attention from a demonized slave-girl. She has become a virtual street-cryer in their behalf, an endorsement Paul hardly cherishes. He finally became so troubled that he turned around and said to the spirit, "In the name of Jesus Christ I command you to come out of her!" At that moment the spirit left her. The exorcism altered the powers of the slave girl to tell fortunes, and so her owners seized Paul and Silas and dragged them before the magistrates.

They found no sympathizes among the crowd, Jew or Gentile. The folks of the city joined the public attack. Paul and Silas had a sagging popularity rating. The magistrates found them guilty, and ordered them to be stripped and beaten. Afterward, they were thrown not only into prison, but placed in the inner cell under strict guard with their feet fastened in irons. The scene, as we noted earlier, is far too common for first century preachers.

At midnight, the two apostles have a prayer meeting. Luke says they "were praying and singing hymns to God and the other prisoners were listening to them." They must have been a curious site – beaten, bloodied, in pain, untreated, with open wounds and every reason to rail at the authorities and complain, instead they sing. They talk to God – to the invisible God. It is no odd thing for us, but in a day of idolatry, talking to an invisible God was a strange thing! "Suddenly there was such a violent earthquake that the foundations of the prison were shaken." God was home, and he answered his mail. The force of the quake is so great that all "at once all the prison doors flew open, and everybody's chains came loose." Notice the idea of liberation again – all doors open, as if by an invisible hand. And everyone's chains come off." That is miraculous. All are freed.

> "The prayers of God's saints are the capital stock in heaven by which Christ carries on his great

work upon the earth. The great throes and mighty convulsions on earth are the results of these prayers. Earth is changed, revolutionized; angels moved on more powerful, more rapid wing, and God's policy is shaped as the prayers are more numerous, more efficient." [42]

The jailer, who had managed not only to ignore the fresh wounds of his newest incarcerated guests, but also to tune out their songs in the night, suddenly woke up. When he discovered the open prison doors, he assumed the worse. They had all escaped. He knew the penalty for his negligence would be death. He preferred suicide. He drew his own sword and was about to kill himself when Paul shouted, "Don't harm yourself! We are all here!" Everyone is free. And everyone should live. What a God. Paul restrains the prisoners from fleeing and thereby putting at risk the life of the jailer. He is not saved because of the dazzling power of God in the earthquake. He is not saved by his exposure to truth. He was interested in the message of Paul and Silas. He did not explore the reasons that put them in his jail. What touched him was neither power or truth. What touched him was love. Their concern for his life. Their willingness to stay in the cell as if they were still chained, so that he would not lose his life – that opened his heart. He took Paul and Silas to his own home, received Christ, was baptized, and became a follower of Jesus Christ.

The power of prayer is a river flowing through the book of Acts. In case you missed the points, let's review them again:

- In Acts 16, prayer looses stocks and bonds, and sets prisoners free.
- In Acts 13, prayer facilitates the operation of spiritual

- gifts and releases the apostolic.
- In Acts 12, prayer is the process by which God chooses to send angels on missions in our behalf, to open the prison doors for Peter. And the resistant King dies there as well.
- In Acts, 6, prayer is the context in which division is healed, the place where we center ourselves.
- In Acts 4, prayer shakes up places where we assemble.
- In Acts 3, prayer invites the miraculous healing power of God.
- In Acts 2, prayer opens a city up to a visitation of God!

There is incredible power in prayer! "God shapes the world by prayer. Prayers are deathless. The lips that uttered them may be closed in death, the heart that felt them may be may have ceased to beat, but the prayers live before God, and God's heart is set on them and prayers outlive the lives of those who uttered them; outlive a generation, outlive an age, outlive a world. That man is the most immortal who has done the most and the best praying."[43]

THE CLOUD

A few years ago, Spencer January went to be with the Lord. I have friends that knew him – knew him as a wonderful Christian man. This is his story:

> It was a morning in early March, 1945, a clear and sunny day. I was 24 years old and a member of the U.S. Army's 35th Infantry Division, 137th Infantry Company I.
>
> Along with several other companies of American troops, we were making our way through dense

woods, towards the Rhine River in the German Rhineland. Our objective was to reach and take the town of Ossenberg, where a factory was producing gunpowder and other products for use in the war.

For hours we had pressed through an unrelenting thicket. Shortly after midday word was passed that there was a clearing ahead. At last, we thought, the going would be easier. But then we approached a large stone house, behind which huddled a handful of wounded, bleeding soldiers who had tried to cross the clearing and failed.

Before us stretched at least 200 yards of open ground, bordered on the far side by more thick woods. As the first of us appeared on the edge of the clearing there was an angry rat-tat-tat and a ferocious volley of bullets sent soil spinning as far as we could see. Three nests of German machine guns, spaced 50 yards apart and protected by the crest of a small hill to the left, were firing across the field. As we got our bearings it was determined that the machine guns were so well placed that our weapons couldn't reach them.

To cross that field meant suicide. Yet, we had no choice. The Germans had blockaded every other route into the town. In order to move on and secure a victory, we had to move forward.

I slumped against a tree, appalled at the grim situation. I thought of home, of my wife and my 5-month old son. I had kissed him good-bye just after he was born. I thought that I might never see my family again, and the possibility was overwhelming.

I dropped to my knees. "God," I pleaded desperately, "You've got to do something. Please do something."

Moments later the order was given to advance. Grasping my M-1 rifle, I go to my feet and started forward. After reaching the edge of the clearing I took a deep breath. But just before I stepped out from cover, I glanced to the left.

I stopped and stared in amazement. A white cloud - a long fluffy white cloud - had appeared out of nowhere. It dropped from over the trees and covered the area. The Germans' line of fire was obscured by the thick foggy mist.

All of us bolted into the clearing and raced for our lives. The only sounds were of combat boots thudding against the soft earth as men dashed into the clearing, scrambling to reach the safety of the other side before the mist lifted. With each step the woods opposite came closer and closer. I was almost across! My pulse pounding in my ears, I lunged into the thicket and threw myself behind a tree.
I turned and watched as other soldiers following me dove frantically into the woods, some carrying and dragging the wounded. This has to be God's doing, I thought. The instant the last man reached safety, the cloud vanished! The day was again bright and clear.

The enemy, apparently thinking we were still pinned down behind the stone house on the other side, must have radioed their artillery. Minutes later the building was blown to bits but our company was safe and we quickly moved on.

Five Basic Prayer Principles

We reached Ossenberg and went on to secure more areas for the Allies. But the image of that cloud was never far from my mind. I had seen the sort of smoke screens that were sometimes set off to obscure troop activity in such situations. That cloud had been different. It had appeared out of nowhere and saved our lives.

Two weeks later, as we bivouacked in eastern Germany, a letter arrived from my mother back in Dallas. I tore open the envelope eagerly. The letter contained words that sent a shiver down my spine. "You remember Mrs. Tankersly from our church?" my mother wrote.

Who could forget her? I smiled. Everybody called Mrs. Tankersly the prayer warrior.

"Well," continued Mom, "Mrs. Tankersly telephoned me one morning from the defense plant where she works. She said the Lord had awakened her the night before at one o' clock and told her, 'Spencer January is in terrible trouble. Get up now and pray for him!"

My mother went on to explain that Mrs. Tankersly had interceded for me in prayer until six o' clock the next morning, when she had to go to her job. "She told me the last thing she prayed before getting off her knees was this "Lord, whatever danger Spencer is in, just cover him with a cloud!"

I sat there for a long time holding the letter in my trembling hand. My mind raced, quickly calculating. Yes, the hours Mrs. Tankersly was praying would indeed have corresponded to the time we were approaching the clearing. With a seven-hour time difference, her prayer for a cloud would have been uttered at one o'clock, the exact time Company I was getting ready to cross the clearing.

From that moment on, I intensified my prayer life. For the past 52 years I have gotten up early every morning to pray for others. I am convinced there is no substitute for the power of prayer and its ability to comfort and sustain others, even those facing the valley of the shadow of death.[44]

There is power in persistent prayer, prayer that is beyond us, bigger than us, prayer by pure-hearted, but less than perfect saintly people, passionate and intense prayer, prayer that we do not even understand, prayer that stretches our perspective of things and calls us into the mysterious ways of God.

Nothing would turn the nation back to God so surely and so quickly as a Church that prayed and prevailed. The world will never believe in a religion in which there is no supernatural power.
A rationalized faith, a socialized Church and a moralized gospel may gain applause, but they awaken no conviction and win no converts.
Samuel Chadwick

Footnotes

1. Bennie S. Triplett, *Praying Effectively* (Cleveland, TN: Pathway Press, 1990), 77-78.
2. This message is taken from: P. Douglas Small *Transformation Themes*, (Chapter Seven, *Prayer*, (Alive Ministries: Kannapolis, NC; May, 2001), 76-87. Published and copyrighted material.
3. www.biblestudytools.com/Dictionaires/BakersEvangelicalDictionary/bed.cgi?number=T732. See Widow, Baker Dictionary.
4. Richard J. Foster *Prayer: Finding the Heart's True Home* (New York: Harper-Collins, 1992), 7.
5. Samuel Chadwick, *The Path of Prayer*, 100.
6. Study by Peter Wagner.
7. Andrew Murray, *God's Best Secrets: An Inspirational Daily Devotional* (Grand Rapids: MI; Kregel Publications, 1993), 45.
8. Mary Ann Bridgwater, Beth Moore, Jerry Rankin, *Prayers for the Faithful: Fervent Daily Prayer and Meditations* (B and H Publishing Group: Nashville, TN; 2008), 428.
9. Ole Hallesby, *Prayer* (Minneapolis: MN: Augsburg Publishing House, 1931; Augsburg Fortress, 1994), 97.
10. J. C. Boyle, quoted by J. I. Packer and Carolyn Nystrom, *Finding Our Way Through Duty to Delight* (Downers Grove, IL: Intervarsity Press, 2006, 2009), 17.
11. Jerry Bridges and Gerald Bridges, *The Chase: Pursuing Holiness in Your Everyday Life* (Colorado Springs, CO; NAV Press, 1993), 11.
12. Bonhoeffer, from *Ethics*, Quoted by Charles Ringma, *Seize the Day with Dietrich Bonhoeffer* (Colorado Springs, Colorado: Pinion Press; 2000), See entry for January 20.
13. Bonhoeffer, from *Letters and Papers from Prison*, Quoted by Charles Ringma, *Seize the Day with Dietrich Bonhoeffer*;

See entry for January 19.
14 Catherine Marshall, *Beyond Our Selves* (Harper Collins Publishers; 1994).
15 Frances Laudrum Tyler. *Pray Ye* (Nashville, TN: Broadman, 1944), 17.
16 Ben Jennings. *The Arena of Prayer* (Orland, Florida: New Life Publications, 1999), 26.
17 Kermit Olsen. *First Steps in Prayer* (New York: Fleming H. Revell; 1947), 56-57. See also; Sir James Jeans. *The Mysterious Universe* (MacMillan), 57.
18 Olsen, 58.
19 Olsen, 27.
20 Charles L. Allen. *All Things are Possible through Prayer* (Grand Rapids, Michigan; 1958, 2003), 101.
21 Robert Schuller. Prayer: *My Soul's Adventure with God* (New York: Image Books; 1995), 216.
22 Lyrics by Joe Darion, from the song: *The Impossible Dream*, and the Musical, *The Man of La Mancha!* www.stlyrics.com/lyrics/bestofbroadway-americanmusical/theimpossibledream.htm.
23 Huston Smith. *Why Religous Matters* (San Francisco: Harper, 2001), 155.
24 Thomas, 149.
25 Jennings, 148.
26 Bonhoeffer, from *Meditating on the Word*, Quoted by Charles Ringma, See entry for January 31.
27 E. M. Bounds, *The Best of E. M. Bounds on Prayer* (Grand Rapids, Michigan: Baker Book House; 1981), 102.
28 Merv Rosell, quoted by Jennings, 151.
29 Jennings, 171-172.
30 T. W. Hunt, *The Doctrine of Prayer* (Nashville, TN: Convention Press; 1986), 91.
31 Frank Laubach. *Prayer – The Mightiest Force in the World* (New York: Fleming H. Revell; 1946), 9-10.

32 Bounds, 11.
33 Allen, 43.
34 William Neil, *The Acts of the Apostles*, 148.
35 William H. Willimon, *Acts*, 112.
36 Longenecker, 410.
37 *Antiquities* 19:339-342.
38 Peter's release from prison and the death of James would have been in the Passover season – March or April, and Herd's sickness would have taken place in August.
39 Josephus observes: *Upon this the king did neither rebuke them, nor reject their impious flattery* (*Antiquities* 19:346).
40 Herod's death is placed in A.D. 44, in the fourth year of the Roman emperor Claudius.
41 www.wcg.org/lit/bible/acts/acts12.htm.
42 Bounds, 76.
43 E. M. Bounds. *The Best of E. M. Bounds on Prayer* (Grand Rapids, Michigan: Baker Book House; 1981), 75.
44 The personal testimony of Spencer January.

projectpray PRODUCTS

DANCING AT THE EDGE OF DARKNESS
If you belong to Christ, your story is "His story!" While non-Christians may be resistant to a canned gospel presentation, your faith neutral friends are open to "your story". Intergenerational story-telling is so important. Your kids need to hear your stories, to see you dancing at the edge of the darkness. (6 CDs) Price: $35

5 LITTLE KNOWN SECRETS OF EFFECTIVE PRAYER: WHY ANYONE CAN PRAY
This is a fascinating message – on sincerity in prayer. The one place you can go with all your disappointment, even your toxic heart, is to God. A message for all those who thought they couldn't pray or didn't know how to pray. (2 CDs) Price: $15

FATHERING AS GOD FATHERS
What makes an effective father? A University study suggest that it is balancing two simple things – love and limits, nurture and control. How does God father? Here are amazing principles on the fathering style of God and their implications for modern fathers. In this journey to Mt. Zion... Sinai and Calvary come together. Price: $15

FOR WOMEN
For those who think the Bible is about a man's world, look again. Here is a study of four women who rocked their world, and changed history. Hannah, a lonely housewife, whose husband brought home another woman, was driven to prayer, and the whole nation pivoted. Rizpah, a social throwaway, Saul's concubine, stood down a king. Mary, the mother of Jesus, journeyed from an angelic visit to the upper room and an unnamed sinner woman taught Simon's dinner guests that real forgiveness was rooted in love. (1 CD; 3 DVDs) Price: $35

MARRIED AND STILL FREE! PLUS—20 IDEAS TO ENRICH FAMILY LIFE
Are you confused about what a Christian marriage looks like? About headship and authority? Doug offers four models for marriage — egalitarian, partnership, authoritarian, and a Biblical model that emphasizes freedom in the context of unity. Also included are twenty practical ideas for enriching family life. (2 CDs) Price: $15

MIRACLES OF ACTS
The first five chapters of Acts are full of miracles! But there is another "miraculous stream" hidden in the text, often completely overlooked. It is the miracle of transformed people living together with great grace. Doug asks; are we emphasizing signs and wonders without adequate attention to the miraculous nature of character? Fire without fruit is not the picture presented in the early chapters of Acts. (3 CDs) Price: $20

POWER OF THANKSGIVING
Thanksgiving is the portal into God's presence. It is the discipline necessary to wake up a cold heart. When we realize all He has done for us is rooted in who He is, our vision of His greatness is renewed. Our problems begin to fade and we move from praise to worship. We are lost in the wonder of who God, our incomparable God, really is. Price: $20

RETHINKING SPIRITUAL WARFARE
This is an alternative view of spiritual warfare – a head-spinning call to rethink all the binding and loosing, all the frontal warfare tactics. Not ignoring the darkness or dismissing the power of the Evil One, Doug carefully works through Biblical passages while suggesting that "wisdom is better than warfare". Our call, he says, is not to spiritual warfare, but to reconciliation of men to God. (2 CDs) Price: $20

SHADOW OVER THE LAND: A LAND DEFILED BY SIN
The shaping issue in the culture today is the one on gender and sexual identity – it threatens family, our view of God, maleness and femaleness. This is not reactionary but a study assessment of the crisis. Why is this such a critical challenge to the church? Why is the topic so spiritually charged? It is more than a mere moral question. The whole of social structure is on the line. In the second CD, Doug reviews the five things that defiled the land in Scripture and what led to the removal of the people from the land. (2 CDs) Price: $15

TEACHING PRAYER EXPERIENCES
You learn to pray—by praying! Jesus took His disciples with Him to pray. He wanted them "to catch" prayer from Him. In these sessions the practical principles of prayer are explored. This includes teaching on prayer and application of those principles. Doug also offers Biblical models for prayer. (4 CDs) Price: $25

THE WOMAN WHO WORSHIPPED HER WAY TO FORGIVENESS
At the home of Simon the Pharisee, a sinner woman crashed the party. She knelt at Jesus' feet and wiped them with her tears. Jesus announced to Simon, that she "was forgiven" because she "loved much". Love, not repentance, as the foundation for forgiveness! Radical. Price: $8

THREE POSITIONS OF PRAYER: BEING CENTERED IN GOD'S LOVE
Luther, the great reformer, prayed, "God, help me!" Doug suggests that such prayers may be from the default mode of our faulty hearts. The heart of prayer is found in God's love for us and our love for Him. Knowing you are loved is the key to knowing you are a conqueror! Prayer centers us in the love of God. (3 CDs) Price: $20

UNEDITED CAMPMEETING EVENTS
Join Doug at various Campmeeting events where he preaches some of his best messages on prayer.
• Let Your Requests Be Known
• 7 Elements of Prayer in a Solemn Assembly
• Intercession the Uncomfortable Strategic Middle
• Prayer Opens Doors
• Entertaining God
(5 CDs) Price: $30

WHAT EVER HAPPENED TO HOLINESS?
Holiness as a concept has disappeared, even in the church. It is misunderstood and caricatured, dismissed and antiquated. It doesn't fit well with a hip hop God or with seeker sensitive evangelicals. Layering a call to righteousness with contemporary data on the state of the church, this is a wake-up call. (3 CDs) Price: $20

TEN CHARACTERISTICS OF A GODLY HUSBAND
A simple and straightforward message from Ephesians 5. Go through the passage and identify Biblical principles aimed at effective partnership. A mixture of humor with serious principles that often determine the success or failure of a marriage. It has simple and profound insights. Price: $15

ANOINTING & MINISTRY OF JESUS
Wherever Jesus went - the power of God flowed out of Him. His promise was clear: "Greater things shall you do! ... These signs shall follow them that believe in my name!" Are their any insights that could help us learn to be more available, more yielded, more of a vessel of the Holy Spirit? It is not technique! It is a heart thing. And yet, there are some principles worth gleaning as we look at the way the anointing flowed in the ministry of Jesus! Price: $20

DOOR OF HOPE IN THE VALLEY OF TROUBLE
The life of Hosea, the prophet, is a metaphor for God's relationship with Israel, with you and me, and by inference, God's relationship with America. When all might have been lost, God leads Israel into the valley of trouble - to renew His relationship with them. This is a powerful message for the Church and a call to national revival. Price: $8

VISIONS OF ZECHARIAH
This is a 4 volume, 16 CD set. Angels are coming and going, horns rise up to scatter the people, wickedness placed in a barrel and exiled to Babylon, carpenters coming to rebuild Jerusalem, the Word of God as a flying scroll pursuing the wicked, the priest purified and then leadership empowered. Wow! This is a template for the renewal of the nation. (Vol. 1, 3 CDs) Price: $20; (Vol. 2, 5 CDs) Price: $30; (Vol. 3, 4 CDs) Price: $25; (Vol. 4, 4 CDs) Price: $25

PRAYER SERIES BOOKLETS
#1 INTERCESSION: THE UNCOMFORTABLE STRATEGIC MIDDLE The first of a new prayer series, Doug shows how Adam was created for the middle—a representative of God in the earth. All creation saw in him the image of God. From that place he fell. Only the last Adam, Jesus, coming to re-secure the broken middle, could reconnect creation to mankind. Jesus came to the middle. Price: $10.95

#2 PRAYER OPENS DOORS This is the second booklet in the prayer series. The whole culture is shutting out the Christian message. Yet, in places previous generations thought unreachable, the doors are blowing open and the church is growing at exponential rates. Verse-by-verse and line-by-line Doug opens the Scripture, calling for renewed dependence on God in prayer. Price: $10.95

DESENSITIZED: THE DANGER OF DESTRUCTIVE BEHAVIOR
You will never think about sin in the same way again - not after this message. Doug tells the story of a young girl who, due to a rare disease, feels no pain and the consequent dangers with which she lives. He suggest that a culture that has desensitized itself and no longer feels moral pain is unaware of the damage they are inflicting on themselves by their destructive behavior. Drawing an analogy between leprosy, Hansen's disease, and sin - he talks about the desensitizing power of sin. Price: CD $8; DVD $15

DISCOVER YOUR DESTINY
A remarkable message about the power of dreams. A god-given dream is not something we make happen, such dreams carry us. God has dreams for us - and so often we settle for much less than his best. This is an encouraging message, especially for those who feel that God might have forgotten or those who sense that somehow their life is off-track. Price: CD $8; DVD $15

BLOOD COVENANT
It is the oldest convenant known to man - apart from marriage. The Blood Covenant. It bound brothers together - to death. It was a pact of brotherhood, of mutuality, of a jointly held oath. It was about loyalty, deep friendship, love and care with pledged action. Could it be that the light and casual fellowship we share as believers is a world away from the blood-brother bonds that God desires us to have with one another? (2 CDs) Price: $15

THE BATTLE OVER THE NAME OF JESUS
Reviews a bit of American history, noting dependence upon God in our early history. Makes a passionate plea to not give up on Jesus, to not move to pluralism as Israel did. In every season, it was in a period in which Israel was flirting with defection to other gods and in such seasons, God showed himself superior and fully alive - to call Israel back to him. Making passionate plea to not compromise the centrality of Jesus in a pluralistic age. As Luther said, "You can sum it all up in the cross!" It's all about Jesus. Price: $15

CHRIST'S RADICAL GOSPEL
In this message, the believer is taken on a journey between love and truth. Some churches today lean to one or the other. Some silence truth when it appears to be unloving or convicting. Others speak truth that isn't tempered with love. The gospel is neither love nor truth, but both bound eternally together. The greatest truth is the love of God. And yet, love without truth is no love at all, only a wrapping for a lie. Love affirms, but truth sets us free. The cross was about God's love, and yet about the truth of sin. Price: CD $8; DVD $15

DREAMS, DESTINY & DISCIPLINE
Every person has a personal destiny! God has a plan for your life! Like Joseph, there are God-given dreams afforded to each of us. However, the manner in which those dreams come to pass are often in ways that confound, confuse and cause us to lose our way. Who could have ever charted the route by which God fulfilled the dreams of Joseph? (2 CDs) Price: $15

THE MEANING OF THE STONES: THE POWER OF YOUR STORY
When your children ask, "What is the meaning of the stones?" All over the land of Israel were stone markers that stood at the site of some great miracle, some deliverance, and some phenomenon that changed an outcome. We need stones that remind us and our children's children of the provision of God, the wonder of His grace. Our stories are dying with us. This is an incredible message on creative, yet ancient ways to share faith. Price: CD $8; DVD $15

PERIMETERS OF CONTROL
In a stunning teaching, Doug shares a simple, but profound concept - setting perimeters of control. A message originally designed for pastors and leaders, this was adapted for a congregation. The principles are the same. The failure to close the doors of our heart to evil, give Satan an advantage. Offers practical advice for setting boundaries that heighten moral fidelity and integrity. A great series for men. Some have called this message a most timely presentation. (4 CDs) Price: $25

ENTERTAINING GOD AND INFLUENCING CITIES
"Prayer is not about words and requests," says Doug Small in *Entertaining God and Influencing Cities*. "It is not even the first and foremost about intercession. That will come. Prayer is about hosting God in a world from which He has been excluded. In prayer, you declare that God is not only welcome, but He is invited . . . you host Him in your heart and your home, the church and your corporation."
Book $14.99; CD $8; DVD $15

EXPLORING ISLAM IN THE LIGHT OF CHRISTIANITY
Five dynamic messages recorded live at Central Church of God (Charlotte, NC) by P. Douglas Small. Topics include: A Spiritual Attack on America; Comparison of the Koran to the Word of God; the Muslim Faith in the Light of the Apostles' Creed; Who is Mohammed? Who is Jesus? (5 CDs) Price: $30

HANNAH: INTIMACY THROUGH ADVERSITY
Hannah was not a powerful and influential figure. Barren, her husband brought home another woman. And Hannah suffered miserably from the depression and conflict. In the loneliness of her own rejection, she turned to God and God gave her a son. The insights she gained by her experience are rare. One lonely housewife, and on the back of her prayer life, the whole nation pivoted. Price: CD $8; DVD $15

HEAVEN IS A COURTROOM ... AN INSIGHT INTO PRAYER
Topics include:
- Three Aspects of Prayer
- Filing Your Petition
- Pleading Your Case
- Integrity
- Building Your Case
- Breakthrough (Intensity in Prayer)

(4 CDs) Price: $25

STUCK IN BETHLEHEM
Stuck in Bethlehem with nothing going right, Mary and Joseph tasted the bitterness of being chosen by God. The ones who are right in the middle of God's will may not be able to see what He is doing. Doug illustrates his message with incidents from the lives of faithful Christians, showing that it is the people who have completely died to themselves that God will use in "Bethlehem's" to give birth to His wonderful purposes. Price: CD $8; DVD $15

SINGING IN THE FACE OF FURY
A contextual study in Revelation! In chapters three and four, Jesus addresses the seven churches of Asia Minor. Among them, only two are not condemned. The condition of the church is appalling – having left its first love, it is doctrinally compromised, it is morally compromised, it is dead . . . it is worse than dead, it is lukewarm. Intoxicated on riches, it is poor and blind. However, instead of finding heaven in a panic, we find it singing. When the church seems to be failing and the geo-political climate becoming more and more godless, we need to join heaven's song.
Price: CD $8; DVD $15

Alive Ministries: Project Pray, P.O. Box 1245, Kannapolis, NC 28082

TRANSFORMING YOUR CHURCH INTO A HOUSE OF PRAYER The sessions cover: Theology of Prayer; Philosophy of Prayer; The Prayer Center; Understanding Mission, Vision & Values; Building a Prayer Leadership Team for Impact; The Discovery Process.
Price: Book $17.99; 3 DVDs $49.99

THE POWER AND PLACE OF GOD'S PRESENCE "Beth" means house. "El" means God. At Bethel, Jacob encountered God's presence. Set up in his dream was a ladder with angels ascending and descending. At the top was God. "This is a dreadful place, a place filled with awe," Jacob would say. "Surely the presence of the Lord is in this place and I knew it not." Bethel, Jacob called it the gateway to heaven. But is it a place? Doug suggests that what Jacob merely dreamed about, Jesus made a reality.
Price: CD $8; DVD $15

RIZPAH: THE WOMAN WHO STOOD DOWN A KING She was a concubine – the property of King Saul. When her sons were cruelly sacrificed to settle a debt, she refused to leave their grave. This is a one-woman crusade. She couldn't bring her sons back, but she made a stand in history showing her love for them and their innocence, and she extracted an apology from a king that changed national policy. This story is of a mother's love, a culturally and legally disenfranchised woman who ignored the boundaries and reversed a 400 year old curse on the nation. Price: CD $8; DVD $15

THE RELATIONAL ORDER OF GOD: APPEAL FOR UNITY Sin is defined in our culture almost exclusively as moral violations of God's holy principles. Lucifer, arguably the number one sinner of all eternity, did not plunge to his depths by first violating the moral order of God. He violated the relational order of God. Unity is not merely a nice thing. It is at the very heart of our Triune God. Church splits, for the noble purpose of beginning a new church, separations and divisions, a lack of genuine agape' love and forgiveness—are all major weapons being effectively used by the Evil One in his spiritual warfare against the Church.
Price: CD $8; DVD $15

THE TABERNACLE Here's a tour of the Tabernacle of Moses – the court, the holy place, the most holy place. Descriptions of the purpose of each piece of furniture – the altar, the laver, the golden table, the lamp stand, the golden altar, the ark of the covenant. Here you find the blood, the water, the bread, the oil, the incense and the glory! It's a template for prayer. A study that goes beyond review of details, this study is rich with spiritual insights.
Price: 4 CD set $25; 2 CD & 2 DVD $35; 2 DVD $25

TOO CLOSE TO THE EDGE Many people frame their Christian choices in terms of right and wrong, heaven and hell. They wonder, "Is this act or attitude a sin? Can I do that, go there, and still keep my faith and relationship with God intact?" They are asking another question, "How close to the edge can I go and still call myself a Christian?" This concept is flawed. The more important question would be "How close can I walk to God?" The right-wrong questions go away when we stop defining our walk in this way and define it in a relational way. Price: CD $8

PRAYER: THE HEARTBEAT OF THE CHURCH Whatever the challenge, conditions, or conflict, prayer has transforming power. Prayer has resurrection power, renewal power, and restoration power. Prayer is the heartbeat of the church! This covers three issues: Magnify the divine privilege of prayer; Motivate individuals to develop a disciplined prayer life; and Mobilize the church to create a prayer culture. As we go forward in prayer, we will witness God's transforming power. Price: Book $10; DVD $15; Devotional $5; Instruction Guide $5; Resource Guide $5

Order by phone
1-8558-4-ALIVE
or
www.alivepublications.org

ALIVE MINISTRIES

NAME _____

ADRESS _____

CITY _____ STATE ____ ZIP _____

PHONE _____

EMAIL _____

○ YES! I would like to be an Alive Ministries INTERCESSOR.

○ YES! I would like to be on Alive Ministries MAILING LIST!

○ YES! I would like to sign up for Alive Ministries CONFERENCES!

PAYMENT INFORMATION

○ Check/Please make check payable to Alive Ministries

○ Credit Card/ Please charge my Credit Card
   Amount: $ _____

Card Type: _____

Name on Card: _____

Card #: _____

Exp. Date: _____

Signature _____

Thank you for your support of Alive Ministries: ProjectPray!!!

THE PRAYING CHURCH MOVEMENT

a network of Church of God Prayer Leaders who affirm the Seven Goals of a Praying Church and are moving toward these goals.

- Receive help with your local church prayer ministry
- Find valuable resources
- Receive advice and counsel
- Connect with fellow believers with a similar passion
- Simultaneously become a part of the Interdenominational Church Prayer Leader's Network

www.praycog.org

Annual Membership Cost:
$30 Registration fee plus
$15 per month or
$150 for the entire year
(paid annually)

P. Douglas Small
*Church of God
Prayer Coordinator*

"The seminar ignited a spirit of prayer in our church."

"I can't believe how this has changed my prayer life."

Host a School of Prayer

Learning About Prayer
- Enriching Your Personal Prayer Life
- Praying Through the Tabernacle
- Prayer the Heartbeat of the Church
- Heaven is a Courtroom

Experiencing Prayer
- The Transformation Prayer Encounter - Learning to Pray by Praying!
- The Prayer Missions Workshop

Praying Leadership
- Transforming the Church into a House of Prayer
- Leading Relaional Prayer Experiences

projectpray

Alive Ministries: **PROJECT PRAY**
PO Box 1245
Kannapolis, NC 28082
www.projectpray.org
1-8558-4-ALIVE

A BRAND NEW INITIATIVE

PRAYER-CONNECT
COMMUNITY LEADERSHIP NETWORK

Have you ever wondered what it would be like to have...

- - - ▶ *a seamless prayer process?*

- - - - - ▶ *all the prayer leaders in your area together at the same table?*

- - - - - ▶ *prayer leaders in your community connected with other communites?*

PC²LN
www.pc2ln.org

Become a part of the Prayer Council Movement.

The Prayer-Connect Leadership Network (PC²LN) is a grassroots group of community prayer leaders who connect, envision, resource and mobilize prayer for a definitive geographic area (town or city).

In conjunction with the National Prayer Committee